Hypothetical City
Workbook III

Hypothetical City Workbook III

Exercises and GIS Data to Accompany
URBAN LAND USE PLANNING, Fifth Edition

Ann-Margaret Esnard, Philip R. Berke,
David R. Godschalk, and Edward J. Kaiser

University of Illinois Press
Urbana and Chicago

Figures 2, 9a, and 9b created with the assistance of Gary Carrington, George Homsy, Karl Mistry, Samantha Robinson, Shannon Schloth, Remington Stone, and Brian Varricchione.

Figures 3, 6a, and 8 created with the assistance of Matthew Flis, Yawen Lu, Dorothy Murray, Allyson Stoll, and Tom Wisemiller.

Figure 5a created with the assistance of Joseph M. Braitsch, Dirk Clinton, Valerie Daley, Rodrigo Godoi, Alyssa Sandoval, and Frank Su.

Figure 5b created with the assistance of Jermaine Gause, Victor Gordon, Anna Karwowska, Chris Ringewald, and Reshmi Theckethil.

Figure 5c and 6b created with the assistance of Leila Aman, Kevin Anderson, Erin Bray, Steven Mikulencak, Giles Patterson, and Fuguang Zhang.

Figure 7 created with the assistance of Helen Chaney, Jeff Grim, Lindy Nelson, and Lindsay Travis.

Figure 10 adapted from Hayseed, Indiana Plan, 2002. Prepared by T3A Planning and Development Consultants (Joshua Abrams, Anthony Fusarelli, Juan Carlos Jimenez, Brian Mings, Adam B. Shindler, and Tama Tochihara).

Contents

Part IV: Notes to Instructor   117

List of Maps

List of Figures

List of Tables

Acknowledgments

We want to thank Professor Richard Klosterman of the University of Akron-Ohio, who coauthored and made substantial contributions to the second edition of the workbook. Joe Stoll (formerly of the University of Akron) and University of North Carolina-Chapel Hill students Karen Berchtold, Dudley Whitney, and XiFang Xing did a considerable amount of work on the original maps, GIS data sets, and spreadsheets. Julie Stein at the University of North Carolina-Chapel Hill facilitated file sharing between the authors. Professor Tim Beatley, University of Virginia, wrote the original version of the simulated public hearing exercise. Leila Aman, a student at Cornell University, assisted with creating all the hard-copy maps and with updating, reviewing, and testing the GIS exercises for this new edition. Robert Koch, also a student at Cornell University, provided useful insight on graphic design tasks.

In addition, we want to thank all our students and teaching assistants who have used the workbook, asked the probing questions, found the flaws, suggested improvements, and generated the quality work represented as illustrative figures in this version of the workbook.

Several colleagues provided excellent feedback on different versions of the workbook: George Frantz, planning consultant and visiting lecturer at Cornell University, who also re-created the streams GIS data layer; Harrison T. Higgins, planner in residence at Florida State University; Professor Robert Olshansky of the University of Illinois at Urbana-Champaign; Professor Susan Roakes at the University of Memphis; and Professor Yan Song at the University of North Carolina-Chapel Hill.

PART I

Purpose and Organization
of the Workbook

This workbook guides the user through the formulation of the components of a future land use plan for a growing small community, and the concepts and methods are applicable to larger cities as well. It provides hands-on experience with land use planning methods and exposure to substantive development-planning issues that tend not to surface until one attempts to apply textbook planning principles. Coping with the projected growth demands of a hypothetical urban area and balancing this against a sustainable community framework and a community's desire to (re)create sustainable land use patterns gives a consistent foundation for organizing and carrying out the sequential tasks of land use plan preparation and for evaluating the resulting package of plan components.

Workbook Purpose

The purpose of this workbook is to support a basic course in land use planning. It includes a set of exercises corresponding to the tasks involved in preparing a future land use plan for a hypothetical city. To facilitate completion of the exercises, the workbook contains the necessary GIS data sets and spreadsheets on an accompanying CD.

This workbook is designed to complement *Urban Land Use Planning, 5th edition,* by Philip R. Berke, David R. Godschalk, and Edward J. Kaiser with Daniel A. Rodriguez (University of Illinois Press 2006). Although the workbook is most effective when readers can refer to the explanations of planning methods provided in *Urban Land Use Planning, 5th edition,* the exercises may also be used on their own in city planning, geography, and urban studies courses that rely primarily on other textbooks.

Workbook materials are organized into four main parts:

- Part I introduces the content of the workbook and explains how to use it.
- Part II describes a hypothetical but realistic town to which the exercises apply.
- Part III outlines a series of basic and supporting land use planning exercises that can be done in various combinations.
- Part IV contains notes to the instructor.

In the real world, situations would obviously be more complicated, data might not be available, political processes would assist or interfere in determining goals and adopting plans, and there would be budget constraints. Nevertheless, the data, maps, tables, and exercises have been tested and modified over several decades and have proven useful for students to learn how to bring data and values to bear in a systematic manner in making a land use plan.

What's New in This Edition

- Complements the fifth edition of *Urban Land Use Planning*
- More illustrative images
- GIS exercise instructions written for ArcGIS (version 8.3 and higher) with useful screenshots to facilitate completion of exercises
- Revised and new data sets on CD (including parcels, roads, water and sewer service boundaries, and streams)
- Updated and new exercises, including:
  - Constructing alternative scenarios for future community development (see Supporting Exercise C)
  - Creating a communitywide Land Use Design (see Exercise 4)
  - Creating a Small-area Plan (see Exercise 5)
  - Land supply and demand acreages by generalized land use categories (Supporting Exercise G, replaces space allocation worktables in previous edition)
  - Plan Quality Evaluation Protocol (see Supporting Exercise I)

Hypothetical City Setting

To do the exercises, the user must become familiar with the urban setting in which the exercises apply. Basic information is contained in Part II, "Description of Hypothetical City." That information includes text, tables, and maps that describe past, present, and projected conditions in the city and its surrounding township.

Users are encouraged to revise the basic factual information in order to customize the workbook's hypothetical urban setting. Several illustrative options are described in Part III, including a postdisaster situation, different economic bases, and geographic locations in various parts of the United States. Going through the process of imagining an alternative urban setting or alternative urban issues challenges the user to work out the connections between the facts, values, and policy directions that make land use planning so complex.

Land Use Planning Exercises

In Part III, the workbook outlines a series of land use planning exercises, divided into two types—basic and supporting. As shown on the left side of Figure 1, the *basic* exercises constitute the primary sequence of land use plan-making tasks.

The basic exercises are supplemented with nine optional supporting and enriching exercises and materials. These supporting exercises are shown on the right side of Figure 1 next to the tasks they supplement.

Just as in actual land use planning practice, the exercises require considerable independent problem solving and they allow much room for creativity. In fact, experimentation with alternative methods and solutions improves the learning experience. The hypothetical city depicted in the workbook can also be given alternative forms and futures by changing growth projections (revising the amount of population growth or the distribution of future employment among industries, for example), or by increasing the significance of environmental constraints (such as a sensitive aquifer-recharge area or an endangered species habitat), stressing particular goals (such as historic preservation or economic development), or placing the community in a different cultural or physical context (such as a mountainous or coastal area). The plans from the various exercises should also be conceived of as products of a multistage process. You can decide to focus on one or more of the types of plans created from Exercises 3 (areawide land policy plan), 4 (communitywide land use design), 5 (small-area plan) and 6 (development-management plan).

Basic Exercises: **Simulating the Sequence of** **Plan-making Stages**	**Supporting Exercises:** **Supporting and Enriching** **the Basic Exercises**
1. Creating a "State of Community" Report	A. Computer Mapping of Existing Conditions B. Conducting a Community Visioning Meeting C. Constructing Alternative Scenarios for Future Community Development
2. Creating a Direction-setting Framework	
3. Creating an Areawide Land Policy Plan	D. Land Suitability Analysis E. Computerized Land Policy District Classification
4. Creating a Communitywide Land Use Design	F. Computerized Land Use Design G. Land Supply and Demand Acreage by Generalized Land Use Categories
5. Creating a Small-area Plan	
6. Preparing a Development-management Program	
7. Evaluating the Plan	H. Plan Review Public Hearing
8. Producing the Complete Plan	I. Critique of Planning Methodology and Plan Quality Evaluation Protocol

Figure 1. Land Use Plan-making Exercises

Hardware and Software Requirements

The main software package required to use several exercises in the workbook is ArcGIS (version 9.1 and higher). The GIS data files provided with the workbook can be used with ArcView (version 2.1 and higher); however, the instructions provided in this edition of the workbook will not be applicable. Workbook users are encouraged to consult ESRI's Web site (www.esri.com) and software manuals for detailed instructions and information on software functionality. If using a server, you must allocate an adequate amount of storage space to students so that GIS data files and projects can be created and saved.

Installation

The GIS data files are contained on a CD that accompanies this workbook. The files are stored in two directories (HYPOCITY and TOWNSHIP) and can be copied fully to a location on your computer. The GIS shapefiles require 5.4 MB of disk space for storage purposes. Detailed instructions for using these files are provided in the discussion of each supporting exercise. Tables 5, 6, 7, 8, and 12 (in Excel spreadsheet format) are also contained on the CD. The files are stored in one directory (TABLES) and can be copied to a location on your computer.

PART II

Description of Hypothetical City

Hypothetical City (Hypo City for short) is a growing urban place of 10,000 people as of 2005, which is assumed to be the current year. It is situated thirty miles west of a metropolis of 250,000 people and fifty miles south of a city of 50,000 people. These base case conditions are elaborated below. Following the base case description, we discuss options for customizing the urban setting in various ways.

Hypo Township has a current population of 11,000 including the 10,000 city residents. It is a rectangle, eight miles wide from east to west, and ten miles long from north to south. It contains eighty square miles, or 51,400 acres. Maps 1 through 14, and the areawide land policy plan exercise, apply to this larger township.

Within the township, the *Hypo City Planning Area* is square, 3.5 miles on a side, with a total area of approximately 12.25 square miles (7,806 acres). The incorporated city comprises approximately 2.5 square miles (approximately 1,696 acres) located approximately in the center of the planning area. The city has extraterritorial planning and growth management jurisdiction over an area of approximately 4.75 square miles outside the city limits, but presently has no land use management jurisdiction over the remaining 5 square miles of the planning area. See Map 18 for delineation of city limits and extraterritorial jurisdiction limits. The planning area is divided into twenty-three planning districts (see Map 20). Planning districts 1 through 7 comprise the existing water-sewer service area and are nearly coincident with the incorporated city limits (there are some small differences along the eastern edge of the city). Maps 15 through 30, and the communitywide land use design, small-area plan, and development-management program exercises apply to this city planning area.

Unless otherwise stated, the data in the tables and text below refer to the planning area of Hypothetical City, not to the larger township area.

Table 1
Population Data

Current (2005) Population

In the township	11,000
In the Hypo City planning area	10,000

Current Number of Households

In the township	3,800
In the Hypo City planning area	3,500
Current average household size	2.9
Median household income	$44,000
Proportion of households below poverty level	12.5%
Township population projected for 2025	22,000
Population growth projected for 2005-2010	2,500
Population growth projected for 2010-2015	3,000
Population growth projected for 2015-2025	5,500

Table 2
Housing Data for Planning Area

Types of Dwellings	Number
Single family, 1–6 du/acre	2,300
Multifamily, 8–20 du/acre	1,400
Total	3,700

House Characteristics	
Vacancy rate	5.4%
Gross density	4.5 du/acre

Tenure	
Owner occupied	55%
Renter occupied	45%

Vacancy rate is calculated by dividing vacant units (200) by total dwellings (3,700). See Table 7 for more information on types and spatial distribution of the current housing stock and Table 8 for information on additions to the housing stock over the last 10 years.

Table 3
Employment Data

SIC*	Industry	Year 2005	Growth	Year 2025
A	Agriculture, Forestry, Fisheries	0	0	0
B	Mining	0	0	0
C	Construction	0	0	0
D	Manufacturing	1,500	1,100	2,600
E	Transportation and Public Utilities	0	0	0
F	Wholesale Trade	800	1,000	1,800
G	Retail Trade	1,000	1,000	2,000
H	Finance and Insurance	100	200	300
I	Services	950	1,150	2,100
J	Unclassified	0	0	0
–	Federal/State Government	0	0	0
–	Local Government	910	1,090	2,000
	Total	5,260	5,540	10,800

* Standard industrial classification code.

Table 4
Current Approximate Employment Densities (employees/acre)

Manufacturing and wholesale	20
Retail and office – central business district (CBD)	55
Retail and office – shopping centers, other	15
Government and other – CBD location	25
Government and other – outside CBD	10

Current floor area in retail uses serving the entire city and the surrounding region is 910,000 square feet, of which 637,000 square feet (70 percent) is in the CBD, 182,000 square feet (20 percent) is in Westgate Shopping Center on the west side of town, and 91,000 (10 percent) is elsewhere. Of the thirty-one acres in commercial use (retail, office, services) in the CBD (not counting parking lots), approximately twenty-seven acres are for establishments serving the entire city and surrounding region; four acres are in retail uses serving the housing in and around the CBD. All retail land use in Westgate Shopping Center is regarded as serving the entire city and surrounding region. It is expected that the need for retail space will grow at approximately the same rate as the population for the township area.

Current floor area in office use is 300,000 square feet, of which 240,000 square feet (80 percent) is in the CBD. Most of the rest of it is in and around Westgate Shopping Center. Population-serving office space is also expected to grow at about the rate of population growth. For headquarters offices, research and development offices, and back-office-type employment and space needs, demand is expected to grow at a rate faster than that of the rest of the economy and faster than population growth; consult employment projections above.

See Map 17 for existing (year 2005) land use in the CBD and Map 19 for existing (year 2005) zoning in the CBD.

Community Facilities

The number and locations of existing community facilities that provide cultural, education, health, and recreation services and supply water and wastewater treatment are shown on Maps 16, 17, 22, and 24. Information about size, capacity, and condition is provided here and in Tables 5, 6, and 9.

The local government has projected the following facility needs over the next twenty years:

• Three elementary schools on ten acres of land each

• Two junior high schools on twenty acres each

• Two community recreation facilities on fifteen acres each

No school or recreation sites have been selected. These need projections are tentative and incomplete. For example, there seem to be no plans for expanding wastewater collection and treatment capacity, which may or may not be a reasonable approach. Projections of community facility needs should be firmed up on the basis of your analyses.

Plans, Regulations, and Policies

Hypo City presently has no written policies, land use plan, or capital improvements program. It has enacted simple subdivision regulations and a simple zoning ordinance; see Map 19. These regulations would normally be considered to remain in place in constructing a "trend-continuation and no-change-in-policy" scenario, but should not be considered a constraint to your planning. That is, you may change the content and spatial pattern of the zoning and subdivision regulations or substitute a different regulatory approach in the development management plan in order to implement your communitywide land use design or areawide land policy plan.

The public water and sewer service district presently coincides approximately with the incorporated city limits. However, it has been the city's policy to extend water and sewer outside city limits "as requested" to new developments, particularly to industrial and commercial development, with the understanding that annexation will follow.

Tables of Data Describing Existing Conditions

Tables 5 through 9 summarize information on existing land use, community facilities, dwellings, vacant land, recent additions to the housing stock, and wastewater treatment capacity for the Hypo City (not the township) planning area. Overviews of the content of the tables are provided below. Hard copy versions of these data tables follow this section of the workbook. Digital versions of Tables 5, 6, 7, and 8 (in Excel spreadsheet format) are provided on the CD that accompanies this workbook. Several of the tables have twenty-three rows, each row representing one of the twenty-three planning districts in the city's planning area. Some tables have information only for the seven districts that represent the area within the incorporated city limits. Refer to Map 20 for the location, boundaries, and pattern of the planning districts.

Table 5. Existing Land Use Acreage by Planning District, Year 2005. The number of acres currently in each of several land uses, with water, or vacant (vacant lots, land in agricultural use or forestry, and fallow land) is shown for each of the twenty-three planning districts.

The industrial-use column includes manufacturing and wholesale trade and employment in plants, warehouses, back offices, and headquarters. Currently, almost all that employment is in plants and warehouses. The commercial-use column includes retail, finance and insurance, and service employment uses, as well as mixed use.

Table 6. Existing Community Facilities, Year 2005. This table indicates the types of facilities in each of the seven districts where such facilities occur. The locations of these facilities are shown on maps 16 and 22.

Table 7. Current Stock of Dwellings, Acreage in Residential Use, and Net Densities by Housing Type, Year 2005. This table shows the number of each of four types of dwellings in each planning district, the acreage taken up by residential uses, and the net density for the district. Totals by dwelling type are at the bottom of the table and the total number of dwellings, total acres in residential use, and average density for each planning district are shown on the right side of the table.

Table 8. Recent Trends in New Additions to Housing Stock, 1995 to 2005. These data come from building permits. They should be taken into consideration when estimating future space requirements for the residential sector.

Table 9. Information about Wastewater Treatment. This table indicates the capacities of the two wastewater treatment plants, the size and holding capacities of their present service areas, the size and maximum build-out population of their gravity sewersheds, and the implied capacity required to serve the build-out level of urbanization.

Table 5
Existing Land Use Acreage by Planning District, Year 2005

Planning District (1)	Total Land (2)	Residential[a] (3)	Industrial (4)	Commercial (5)	Community Facilities (6)	Recreational (7)	Other (Medical) (8)	Transport. (9)	Total Developed (10)	Water (11)	Vacant (12)
Central City											
1	121	24	9	31	12	0	0	21	97	0	24
2	82	30	10	0	6	0	0	10	56	0	26
3	229	80	0	5	7	22	0	22	136	0	93
4	542	140	109	0	9	12	6	63	339	0	203
5	324	169	0	33	16	8	11	55	292	0	32
6	197	92	0	0	6	27	0	25	150	26	21
7	201	76	0	5	16	8	0	20	125	0	78
Subtotal	**1,696**	**611**	**128**	**74**	**72**	**77**	**17**	**216**	**1,195**	**26**	**477**
Fringe Area											
8	351	25	0	0	0	0	0	7	32	0	319
9	447	44	0	0	0	0	0	11	55	0	392
10	282	28	0	0	0	0	0	14	42	0	240
11	94	0	0	0	0	0	0	16	16	0	78
12	110	16	0	0	0	0	0	16	32	0	78
13	390	16	0	0	0	0	0	16	32	0	358
14	453	10	0	0	0	0	0	22	32	48	373
15	270	6	0	0	0	0	0	27	33	0	237
16	596	35	0	0	0	0	0	29	64	0	532
17	555	0	0	0	0	0	0	4	4	0	551
18	376	0	0	0	0	0	0	4	4	51	321
19	372	9	0	0	0	0	0	6	15	0	357
20	438	19	0	0	0	0	0	13	32	0	406
21	766	9	0	0	0	0	0	26	35	0	731
22	322	0	0	0	0	0	0	0	0	0	322
23	288	0	0	0	0	0	0	0	0	0	288
Subtotal	**6,110**	**217**	**0**	**0**	**0**	**0**	**0**	**211**	**428**	**99**	**5,583**
Total	**7,806**	**828**	**128**	**74**	**72**	**77**	**17**	**427**	**1,623**	**125**	**6,060**

a. Same as total acres (column 15) in Table 7.

Table 6
Existing Community Facilities, Year 2005

Planning District (1)	Elementary Schools Number (2)	Acres (3)	Junior High Schools Number (4)	Acres (5)	Senior High Schools Number (6)	Acres (7)	Parks with Rec. Facilities Number (8)	Acres (9)	Other Facility (10)	Acres (11)
1	0	0	0	0	0	0	0	0	City hall	3
									Courthouse	7
									Library	2
2	0	0	0	0	0	0	0	0	Sewage plant	6
3	1	7	0	0	0	0	2	22		0
4	1	9	0	0	0	0	1	12	Nursing home	6
5	0	0	0	0	1	16	1	8	Hospital	11
6	1	6	0	0	0	0	2	53[a]		0
7	0	0	1	10	0	0	2	8	Sewage plant	8
Total	**3**	**22**	**1**	**10**	**1**	**16**	**8**	**103**		**43**

a. Includes a 26-acre lake.

Table 7

Current Stock of Dwellings, Acreage in Residential Use, and Net Densities by Housing Type, Year 2005

Planning District (1)	Single-family Detached[a]			Row/Townhouses[b]			Garden Apartments[c]			Multistory Apartments			Total		
	DUs (2)	Acres (3)	Density (4)	DUs (5)	Acres (6)	Density (7)	DUs (8)	Acres (9)	Density (10)	DUs (11)	Acres (12)	Density (13)	DUs (14)	Acres (15)	Density (16)
Central City															
1	120	20	6.0	0	0		10	2	5.0	40	2	20.0	170	24	7.1
2	105	20	5.3	25	3	8.3	25	2	12.5	100	5	20.0	255	30	8.5
3	135	43	3.1	200	17	11.8	250	16	15.6	75	4	18.8	660	80	8.3
4	420	103	4.1	300	23	13.0	225	13	17.3	0	0		945	140	6.8
5	675	169	4.0	0	0		0	0		0	0		675	169	4.0
6	345	92	3.8	0	0		0	0		0	0		345	92	3.8
7	215	66	3.3	100	7	14.3	50	3	16.7	0	0		365	76	4.8
Subtotal	**2,015**	**513**	**3.9**	**625**	**50**	**12.5**	**560**	**36**	**15.6**	**215**	**11**	**19.5**	**3,415**	**611**	**5.6**
Fringe Area															
8	60	25	2.4	0	0		0	0		0	0		60	25	2.4
9	55	44	1.3	0	0		0	0		0	0		55	44	1.3
10	30	28	1.1	0	0		0	0		0	0		30	28	1.1
11	0	0		0	0		0	0		0	0		0	0	0.0
12	25	16	1.6	0	0		0	0		0	0		25	16	1.6
13	15	16	0.9	0	0		0	0		0	0		15	16	0.9
14	10	10	1.0	0	0		0	0		0	0		10	10	1.0
15	5	6	0.8	0	0		0	0		0	0		5	6	0.8
16	45	35	1.3	0	0		0	0		0	0		45	35	1.3
17	0	0		0	0		0	0		0	0		0	0	0.0
18	0	0		0	0		0	0		0	0		0	0	0.0
19	10	9	1.1	0	0		0	0		0	0		10	9	1.1
20	20	19	1.1	0	0		0	0		0	0		20	19	1.1
21	10	9	1.1	0	0		0	0		0	0		10	9	1.1
22	0	0		0	0		0	0		0	0		0	0	0.0
23	0	0		0	0		0	0		0	0		0	0	0.0
Subtotal	**285**	**217**	**1.3**	**0**	**0**	**0**	**0**	**0**	**0**	**0**	**0**	**0**	**285**	**217**	**1.3**
Total	**2,300**	**730**	**3.2**	**625**	**50**	**12.5**	**560**	**36**	**15.6**	**215**	**11**	**19.5**	**3,700**	**828**	**4.5**

Notes: a. Single-family detached housing could be split into several density classes.
b. Attached housing includes duplexes, townhouses, and row houses.
c. Ground-floor and walk-up apartments.

Table 8
Recent Trends in New Additions to Housing Stock, 1995 to 2005

| Planning District (1) | Total Number DUs Added in Zone (2) | Percentage of Planning Area Total (3) | Conversions (4) | New Construction by Housing Type | | | | | | Total (11) |
| | | | | Single-family Detached | | | Multifamily | | | |
				Low Density (<1 DU/acre) (5)	Med. Density (1–3 DU/acre) (6)	High Density (3–6 DU/acre) (7)	Attached Duplexes, Townhouses (8)	Garden Apts. (9)	Multistory Apts. (10)	
Central City										
1	20	2.0	10	0	0	10	0	0	0	10
2	42	4.1	0	0	0	12	15	15	0	42
3	150	14.7	10	0	0	15	0	50	75	140
4	320	31.4	0	35	50	65	70	100	0	320
5	250	24.5	0	70	130	50	0	0	0	250
6	75	7.4	0	10	45	20	0	0	0	75
7	100	9.8	10	0	0	30	10	50	0	90
Subtotal	**957**	**93.8%**	**30**	**115**	**225**	**202**	**95**	**215**	**75**	**927**
Fringe Area										
8	30	2.9%	0	10	10	10	0	0	0	30
9	5	0.5%	0	0	5	0	0	0	0	5
10	2	0.2%	0	0	2	0	0	0	0	2
11	3	0.3%	0	0	0	3	0	0	0	3
12	0	0.0%	0	0	0	0	0	0	0	0
13	3	0.3%	0	0	3	0	0	0	0	3
14	5	0.5%	0	0	5	0	0	0	0	5
15	5	0.5%	0	3	2	0	0	0	0	5
16	10	1.0%	0	5	5	0	0	0	0	10
17	0	0.0%	0	0	0	0	0	0	0	0
18	0	0.0%	0	0	0	0	0	0	0	0
19	0	0.0%	0	0	0	0	0	0	0	0
20	0	0.0%	0	0	0	0	0	0	0	0
21	0	0.0%	0	0	0	0	0	0	0	0
22	0	0.0%	0	0	0	0	0	0	0	0
23	0	0.0%	0	0	0	0	0	0	0	0
Subtotal	**63**	**6.2%**	**0**	**18**	**32**	**13**	**0**	**0**	**0**	**63**
Total	**1,020**	**100.0%**	**30**	**133**	**257**	**215**	**95**	**215**	**75**	**990**
Percentage by Housing Type		100.0%	2.9%	13.0%	25.2%	21.1%	9.3%	21.1%	7.4%	97.1%

Table 9
Information about Wastewater Treatment

	North Creek Plant (Plan. District 1, 5, 6, 7)	South Creek Plant (Plan. District 1, 2, 3, 4)
Present Capacity		
Amount of Wastewater	1.2 m.g.d.	1.0 m.g.d.
Equivalent Population[a]	9,600	8,000
Size of Present Service District		
Acreage	773[b]	963[c]
Population	3,800	5,500
Size of Potential Service District		
Acreage	1,660[d]	2,126[e]
Build-out Population[f]		
Future	9,000	10,900
Existing	3,800	5,500
Total	12,800	16,400
Implied Required Capacity of Plant at Build-out	1.6 m.g.d.	2.1 m.g.d.

a. Calculated at 125 gallons per capita per day.

b. Approx. sum of acres: planning districts 5, 6, 7 + part of planning district 1.

c. Approx. sum of acres: planning districts 2, 3, 4 + part of planning district 1.

d. Approx. sum of acres: 733 + planning districts 8, 16 + part of planning district 15.

e. Approx. sum of acres: 963 + planning districts 12, 13, 14 + part of planning district 15.

f. Calculated as though entire sewershed were built out at the existing citywide gross density of Hypothetical City, which is 2.8 dwellings per acre. It also assumes continuation of the current household size of 2.9, and assumes a 5 percent vacancy rate. Changes in any of these assumptions will change the build-out population capacity and implied required capacity of the wastewater treatment plants at build-out. The citywide gross density allows for commercial, industrial, and mixed-use development as well as open space and community facilities in the same proportions as now exist in Hypothetical City.

Maps of Existing Conditions

Maps 1 through 30 describe the spatial distribution of various features of Hypo Township and Hypo City. Hard copy versions are located at the end of this part of the workbook, and GIS data files are provided on the accompanying CD. These GIS data files should have been copied onto your hard disk (in the folder you specified). These installation procedures are described in the section called "Installation" in Part I.

Maps 1 through 14 are of the *township* planning area (used primarily for the areawide land policy district plan exercise and supporting exercises). Maps 15 through 30 cover the *city's* planning area. The *GIS files for the township area maps* are listed in Table 10. This table contains the GIS file name, the map number, a description of the map content, the classification field, and the classification categories. The *GIS files for the city area maps* are listed in Table 11. This table contains the GIS data file name, the map number, a description of the map content, the classification field, and the classification categories. For example, Map 25, with the file name *Agricult* and with the classification field name *Agricultur*, contains land suitable for agricultural use.

Township Planning-area Maps

Map 1. Existing Roads (township planning area). The map indicates the interstate bypass on the south side of the city, the thoroughfares (north-south highway and east-west highway that intersect in the CBD; highways leading off to the northwest, southwest, and southeast), and the network of local streets that provide access to properties and some outlying areas.

Map 2. Drainage Boundaries and Streams (township planning area). Note the area that drains into the city's water-supply reservoir north of the city. The map also shows streams and the sewersheds (i.e., the area within which wastewater will flow by gravity to each of the two treatment plants). This map was created from two GIS data files (included on the CD): *Drainage & Streamst.*

Map 3. 100-Year Floodplains (township planning area). The four categories are floodplain, lake, nonflood land, and reservoir.

Map 4. Prime Agricultural Lands (township planning area). The four categories are prime agricultural land, lake, other, and reservoir.

Map 5. Poor Soil Percolation (township planning area). The two soil suitability classes for on-site wastewater treatment are good and poor. Soils categorized as poor (i.e., ill-suited for on-site wastewater treatment) are generally not suitable for low-density residential development.

Map 6. Slopes (township planning area). The three slope categories represented in this map are 0-5%, 6-15%, and >15%. These three categories of slope correspond to fairly widely accepted slope limits for certain types of development in many parts of the United States. Steeper slopes are ill-suited for dense housing and commercial and industrial development. The slope intervals indicated on the map may be changed, however, to reflect the accepted limits in other regions or countries.

Map 7. Forest Lands (township planning area). The three forest covers represented in this map are lowland-hardwood, pine, and upland-hardwood.

Map 8. Buffer Distances from CBD (township planning area). This map represents buffer distances from the CBD in 0.5 mile increments, up to 7.0 miles.

Map 9. Buffer Distances from Commercial Centers (township planning area). The six categories of buffer distance from existing commercial centers are 0-0.5 mile (same as 0-2,640 feet), 0.5-1 mile, 1-2 miles, 2-3 miles, 3-4 miles, and >4 miles.

Map 10. Buffer Distances from Sewer Lines (township planning area). The six buffer distances represented in this map are 0-500 feet, 500-2,640 feet, 0.5-1 mile, 1-2 miles, 2-3 miles, and >3 miles. See Map 24 for the location of the existing sewer lines.

Map 11. Buffer Distances from Reservoir and Tributary Streams (township planning area). This map represents three buffer distances from the water supply reservoir, 0-500 feet, 500-1,320 feet, and >1,320 feet.

Map 12. Buffer Distances from Interstate Highway (township planning area). This map represents buffer distances from the interstate in 0.5 mile increments.

Map 13. Current Urban Development. This map delineates current urban development based on three criteria: developed, undeveloped, and water. Please note that this is not at all the same as what the student will want to define as a "developed" land policy district in the areawide land policy district plan.

Map 14. Land Classification Overlay. This map is an overlay of maps 1-13. It is an essential map for the computer-based suitability analysis (described in Supporting Exercise D) and computerized land policy district classification (described in Supporting Exercise E). It allows the user to select various combinations of land uses and characteristics, such as prime agricultural land with poor soil percolation and on steep slopes.

Table 10

Names and Descriptions for Hypo Township GIS Data Files

GIS File Name	Map No.	Description	Classification Field	Classification/Categories
Agricult	4	Prime Agricultural Lands	Agricultur	Land suitable for agricultural use: "agriculture," "reservoir," "lake," and "others"
Allroads	1	Existing Roads	Roadtype	Existing roads: "road," "interstate," and "railroad"
Cbdbuff	8	Buffer Distances from CBD	Cbdbuf	Buffer distance from CBD in 0.5 mile increments (14 categories)
Commbuf	9	Buffer Distances from Commercial Centers	Commbuf	Buffer distance from existing commercial centers (6 categories): "0-2,640 ft.," "0.5-1 mi.," "1-2 mi.," "2-3 mi.," "3-4 mi.," and ">4 mi."
Develop	13	Current Urban Development	Develop	Current urban development: "developed," "undeveloped," and "water"
Drainage & Streamst	2	Drainage Boundaries and Streams	Drainage	Sewersheds for two existing sewage treatment plants: "ridge lines," "sewershed limits," and "streams"
Flood	3	100-Year Floodplains	Flood	Floodplain and water areas: "floodplain," "reservoir," "lake," and "other/nonflood land"
Forest	7	Forest Lands	Forest	Forest covers: "pine," "lowland hardwood," "upland hardwood," and "other"
Hywbuf	12	Buffer Distances from Interstate Highway	Hywbuf	Distance from interstate in 0.5 mile increments (6 categories)
Sewerbuf	10	Buffer Distances from Sewer Lines	Sewerbuf	Distances to existing sewer system: "0-500 ft.," "500-2,640 ft.," "0.5-1 mi.," "1-2 mi.," "2-3 mi.," and ">3 mi."
Slopes	6	Slopes	Slope	Land slope: "0-5%," "6-15%," and ">15%"
Soils	5	Poor Soil Percolation	Soils	Soil suitability for on-site wastewater treatment: "poor" and "good"
Waterbuf	11	Buffer Distances from Reservoir and Tributary Streams	Waterbuf	Distance from the lake: "0-500 ft.," "500-1,320 ft.," ">1,320 ft."

Note: 1 mile = 5,280 feet.

City Planning-area Maps

Map 15. Existing Roads. The map indicates the interstate bypass (on the south side of the city), the thoroughfares (north-south highway and east-west highway that intersect in the CBD; highways leading off to the northwest, southwest, and southeast), and the network of local streets that provide access to properties and some outlying areas.

Map 16. Existing Land Uses. The land use map is generated from the parcel GIS data layer and shows present land use in the city (see Table 11 for categories and classification field). Note that there is vacant land within the city limits, even within what looks like built-up residential, industrial, and commercial areas on the map. Some vacant land is probably suitable for infill development. The amount of vacant land in each planning district is indicated in Table 5.

Map 17. Existing Land Use in the CBD. This map is the same as Map 16, but zoomed into the CBD.

Map 18. Existing Zoning and Extraterritorial Jurisdiction Limits. The zoning map is generated from the parcel GIS data layer (see Table 11 for categories and classification field). Extraterritorial powers for land use controls (e.g., zoning and subdivision regulations) extend 0.5 mile beyond the present city limits. Zoning does not exist in the township beyond the extraterritorial limits. Note that there are discrepancies between present zoning and present land use, especially in and around the CBD. Also, there is vacant land in areas zoned for urban uses. It is a factor that can be changed in the development-management plan in Exercise 6, however, and should not constrain the land use plan.

Map 19. Existing Zoning in the CBD. This map is the same as Map 18, but zoomed into the CBD. Note that some present uses (seen in this map) do not conform with zoning, having been established before the zoning was adopted.

Map 20. Planning Districts. The city's planning area is divided into twenty-three planning districts. Many of the tables describing Hypo City organize data by these planning districts. District boundaries follow prominent edges such as ridge lines, city limits, and major highways, and are drawn so that the districts are relatively homogeneous.

Map 21. Current Urban Development. This map is generated from the parcel GIS data layer (see Table 11 for categories and classification field). This map delineates current urban development based on three criteria: developed, undeveloped, and water. Please note that this is not at all the same as what the student will want to define as a "developed" policy district in the areawide land policy plan.

Map 22. Location of Public Services. This map is generated from the parcel GIS data layer (see Table 11 for categories and classification field). The location of public services such as the city hall, schools, library, hospital, and so on are represented on this map.

Map 23. Slopes. The three slope categories represented in this map are 0-5%, 6-15%, and >15%. These three categories of slope correspond to fairly widely accepted slope limits for certain types of development in many parts of the United States. Steeper slopes are ill-suited for dense housing and commercial and industrial development. The slope intervals indicated on the map may be changed, however, to reflect the accepted limits in other regions or countries.

Map 24. Sewer Utility Factors. The reservoir north of the city is the only water supply; two bays of that reservoir appear along the northern edge of the city's planning area. Maps 2 and 3 show the entire reservoir in relation to the city. There are two sewage treatment plants on the eastern edge of the city. One treats sewage from the northern part of the city and the other the southern part. A ridge line runs east and west through the center of the city dividing the northern sewershed from the southern sewershed. Drainage within the sewersheds is generally from west to east, so that areas to the east of the treatment plants are downhill from the plants and cannot be served by gravity sewer. For those areas to be sewered, sewage would have to be pumped upstream to the existing plants or a new plant or plants must be built downstream (to the east). Lands to the west of the sewage treatment plants are uphill and can be sewered by gravity sewer, up to the ridge lines. There is land beyond the ridge lines in the northern, southern, and eastern part of the planning area that lies beyond the existing sewersheds. Urban development in those areas would require either pumping sewage up to the ridge line or alternative treatment facilities, such as treatment plants in new watersheds. Information about the capacity of the sewage treatment plants is contained in Table 9. This map was created from five GIS data files (all included on the CD): *citysquare, drainage, sewers, streamsc, and watsewb.*

The present public water and sewer service district corresponds roughly to the city limits and includes planning districts 1 through 7. The existing service area and additional areas that can be serviced most economically are important considerations in formulating the areawide land policy plan and the communitywide land use design.

Map 25. Prime Agricultural Lands. The areas indicated as "prime agricultural land" are the most fertile for agricultural production. Users may add other environmental resources, change the pattern of prime agricultural land, or assume that the environmental resource represented is something other than prime agricultural land (e.g., national forest).

Map 26. Poor Soil Percolation. The areas indicated as "poor soil percolation" contain soils that pose problems for on-site wastewater treatment systems (septic tanks), generally required for low-density development on the urban fringe.

Map 27. Distribution of Socioeconomic Classes. This map shows the location of six different socioeconomic classes: low, lower-middle, transition, middle, upper-middle, and upper.

Map 28. 100-Year Floodplains. The 100-year floodplain is mapped along the two creeks and a few other places in the planning area subject to flooding. Users may add other natural hazards or environmentally sensitive lands, such as wetlands.

Map 29. Buffer Distances from the CBD (city planning area). This map represents buffer distances from the CBD in 0.5 mile increments (up to 3 miles).

Map 30. Drainage Boundaries and Streams (city planning area). The map also shows the sewersheds—the area within which wastewater will flow by gravity to each of the two treatment plants. This map was created from two GIS data files (included on the CD): *Drainage* and *Streamsc.*

Table 11
Names and Descriptions for Hypo City GIS Data Files

File Name	Map No.	Description	Classification Field	Classification/Categories
Agricult	25	Prime Agricultural Lands	Agricultur	Land suitable for agricultural use: "agriculture" and "other"
Cbdbuff	29	Buffer Distances from the CBD	Cbdbuf	Buffer distance from CBD in 0.5 mile increments (6 categories)
Cityroad	15	Existing Roads	Roadtype	Existing roads: "road," "interstate," and "railroad"
Drainage & Streamsc	30	Drainage Boundaries and Streams	Drainage	Sewersheds for two existing sewage treatment plants: "ridge lines," "sewershed limits," and "streams." See description for a list of all the files used to create the map.
Flood	28	100-Year Floodplains	Flood	Floodplain and water areas: "nonflood land," "floodplain," "reservoir," and "lake"
Parcel	21	Current Urban Development	Develop	Current urban development: "developed," "undeveloped," and "water"
Parcel	16 17	Existing Land Uses Existing Land Use in the CBD	Landuse	Existing land use: "water," "residential," "commercial," "community facilities," "recreational," "industrial," "open space," "transportation," "vacant," and "others"
Parcel	22	Location of Public Services	Service	Location of public services: "city hall," "E school," "Jr. H school," "Sr. H school," "hospital," "lake," "library," "nursing home," "park," "reservoir," wastewater," and "train station"
Parcel	18 19	Existing Zoning and Extraterritorial Jurisdiction Limits Existing Zoning in the CBD	Zoning	Zoning for each parcel: "commercial," "industrial," "institutional," "low-density residential," "high-density residential," "transportation," "water," and "no zoning"
Plandist	20	Planning Districts	Plandist	Planning district number
Sewers	24	Sewer Utility Factors	Sewers_id	Location of existing sewer lines. See description section for a list of the files used to create the map.
Slopes	23	Slopes	Slope	Land slope: "0-5%," "6-15%," and ">15%"
Socio	27	Distribution of Socioeconomic Classes	Socio	Location of six different socioeconomic classes: "low," "lower-middle," "transition," "middle," "upper-middle," and "upper"
Soils	26	Poor Soil Percolation	Soils	Soil suitability for on-site wastewater treatment: "poor" and "good"

Interstate
Railroad
Road
Thoroughfare

Feet
0   3,000   6,000

Map 1 Existing Roads

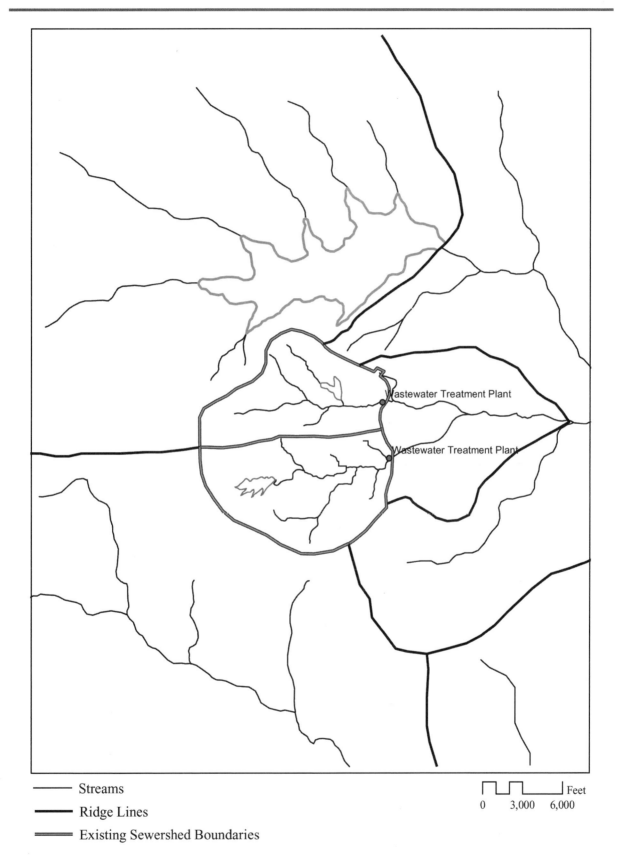

Wastewater Treatment Plant

Wastewater Treatment Plant

——— Streams

——— Ridge Lines

——— Existing Sewershed Boundaries

Feet

0   3,000   6,000

Map 2 Drainage Boundaries and Streams

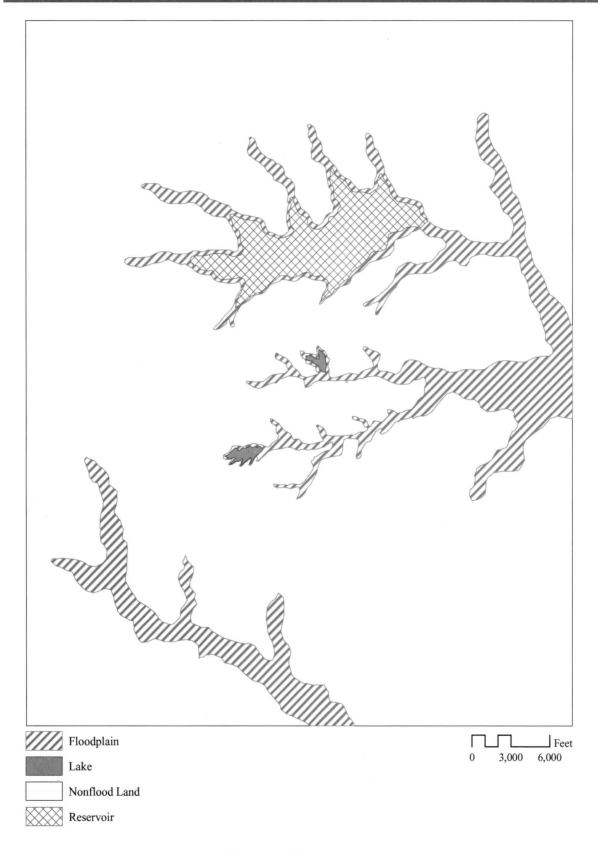

Map 3   100-Year Floodplains

Prime Agricultural Land	
Lake	
Other	
Reservoir	

Feet

0   3,000   6,000

Map 4 Prime Agricultural Lands

Good Soil Percolation

Poor Soil Percolation

0   3,000   6,000 Feet

Map 5 Poor Soil Percolation

0-5%

6%-15%

>15%

Water

Fee

0   3,000   6,000

Map 6 Slopes

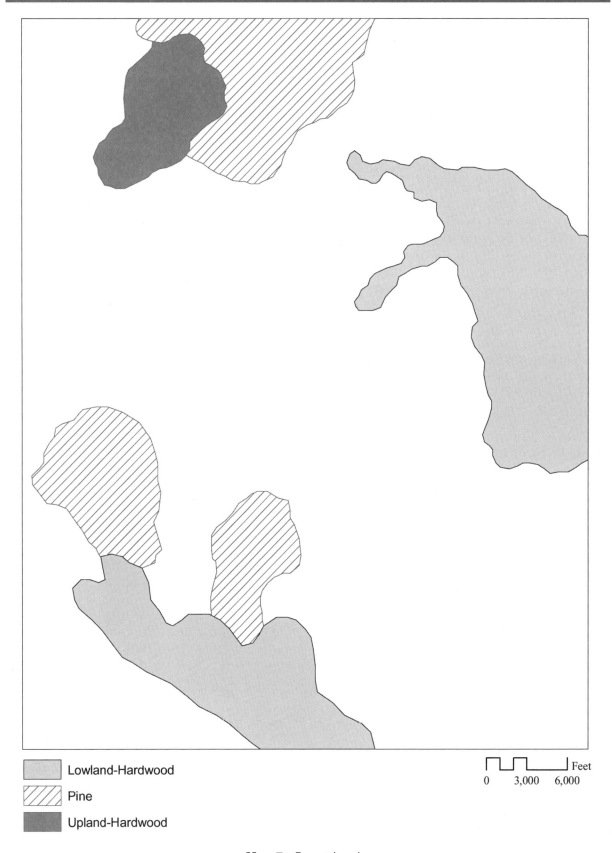

Lowland-Hardwood

Pine

Upland-Hardwood

Feet

0   3,000   6,000

Map 7 Forest Lands

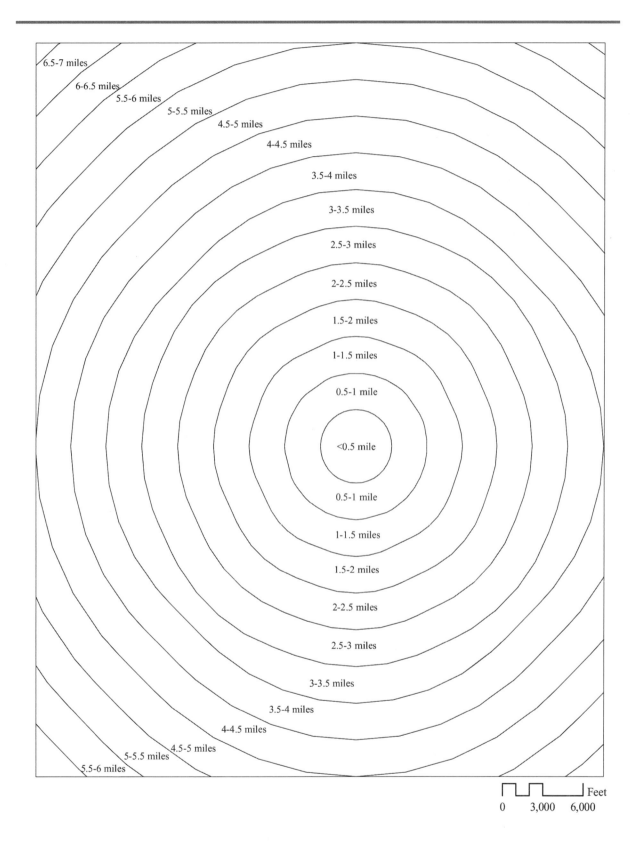

Map 8 Buffer Distances from CBD

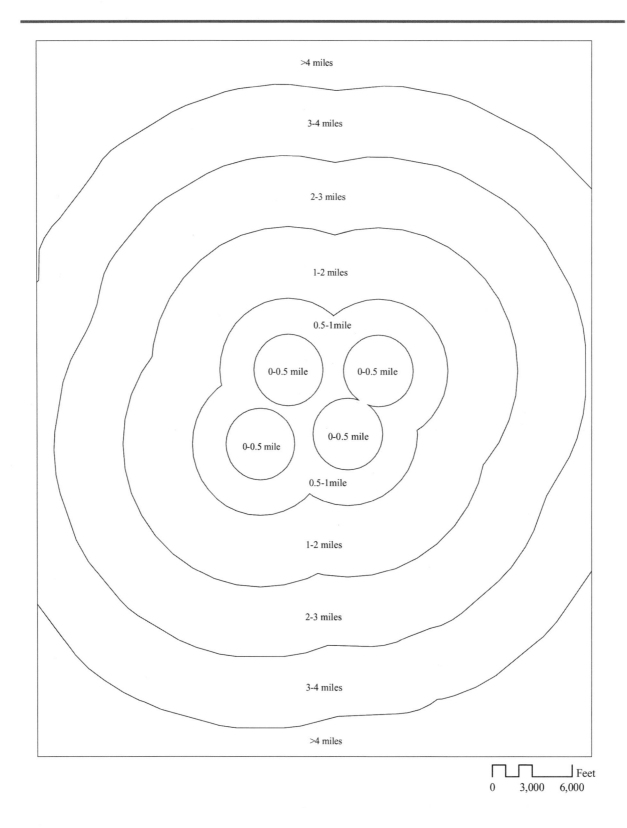

Map 9 Buffer Distances from Commercial Centers

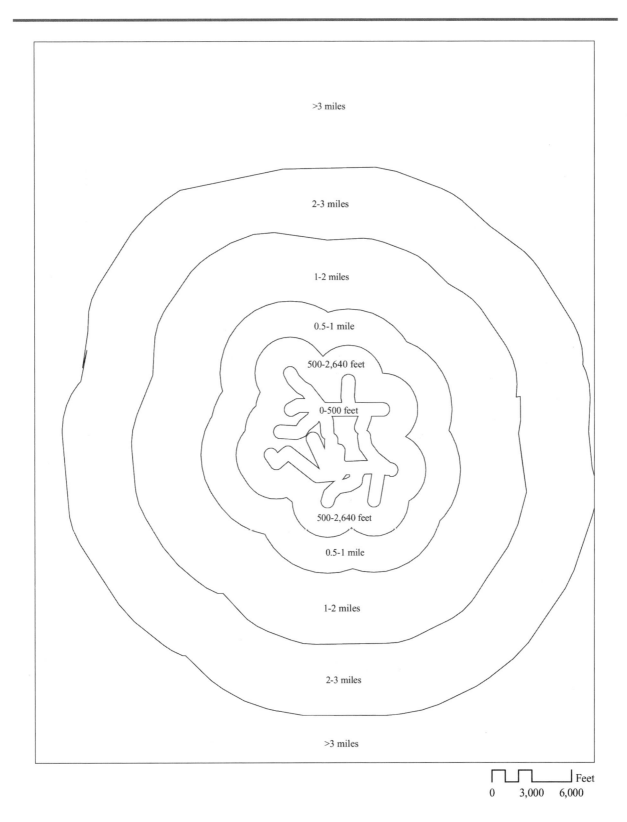

>3 miles

2-3 miles

1-2 miles

0.5-1 mile

500-2,640 feet

0-500 feet

500-2,640 feet

0.5-1 mile

1-2 miles

2-3 miles

>3 miles

Feet
0   3,000   6,000

Map 10   Buffer Distances from Sewer Lines

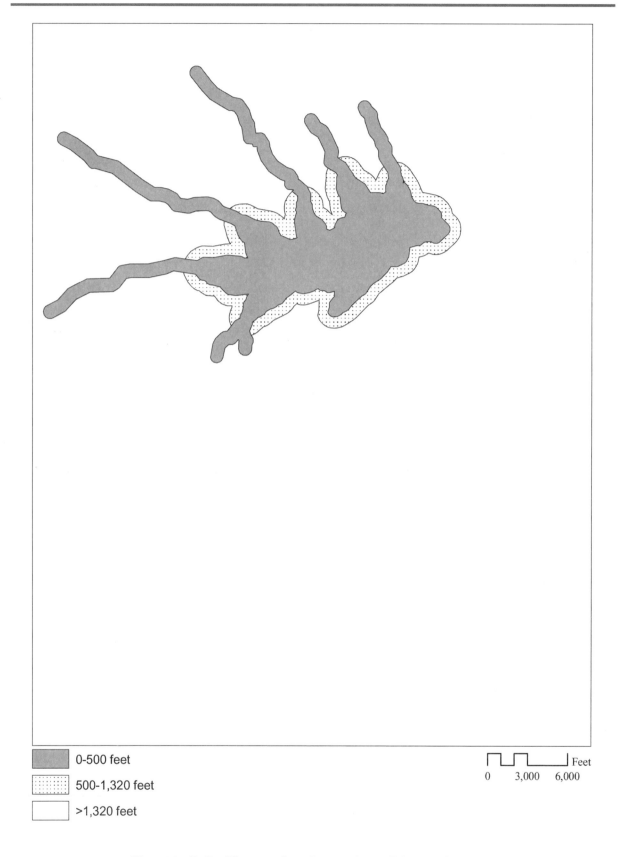

▓	0-500 feet
░	500-1,320 feet
□	>1,320 feet

Map 11   Buffer Distances from Reservoir and Tributary Streams

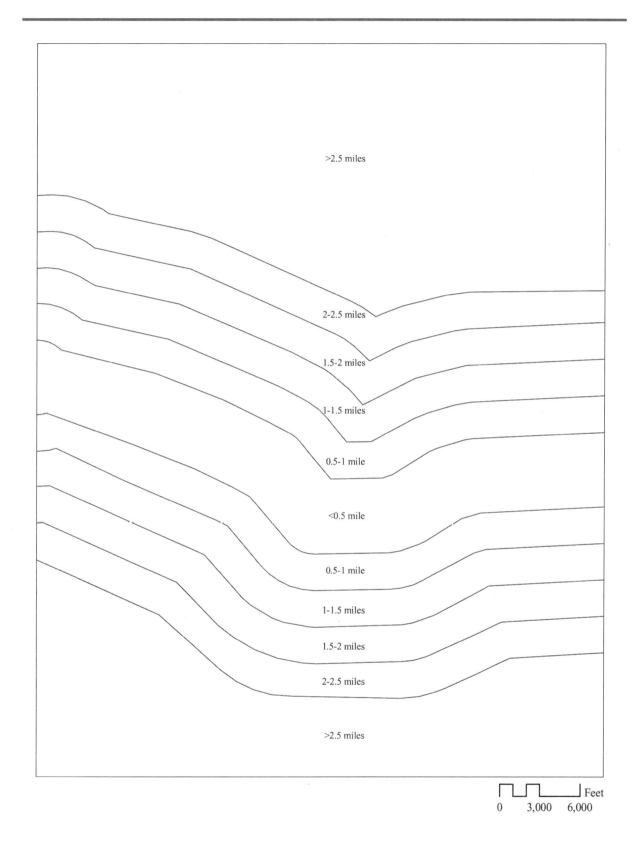

Map 12 Buffer Distances from Interstate Highway

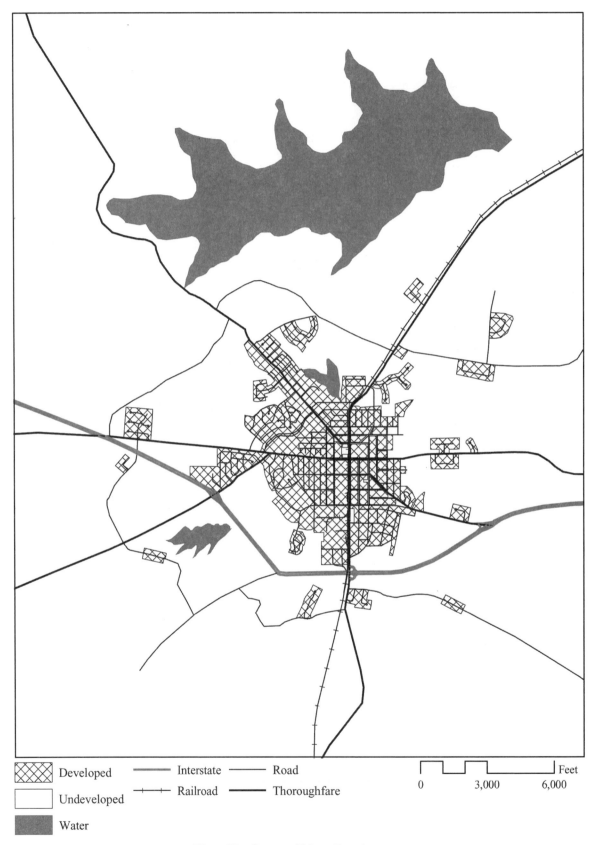

⊠ Developed	▬▬ Interstate	── Road	
☐ Undeveloped	┼─┼─┼ Railroad	▬▬ Thoroughfare	
■ Water			

0   3,000   6,000 Feet

Map 13 Current Urban Development

Map 14 Land Classification Overlay

Interstate
Railroad
Road
Thoroughfare

Feet
0   1,500   3,000   6,000

Map 15 Existing Roads

■ Commercial	▨ Recreational		
▩ Community Fac.	░ Residential		
▧ Industrial	┆ Transportation		
□ Open Space	▪ Vacant		
░ Others	▬ Water		

0   1,500   3,000   6,000   Feet

Map 16 Existing Land Uses

Commercial

Community Fac.

Industrial

Open Space

Others

Recreational

Residential

Vacant

Water

Feet

0   375   750   1,500

Map 17 Existing Land Use in the CBD

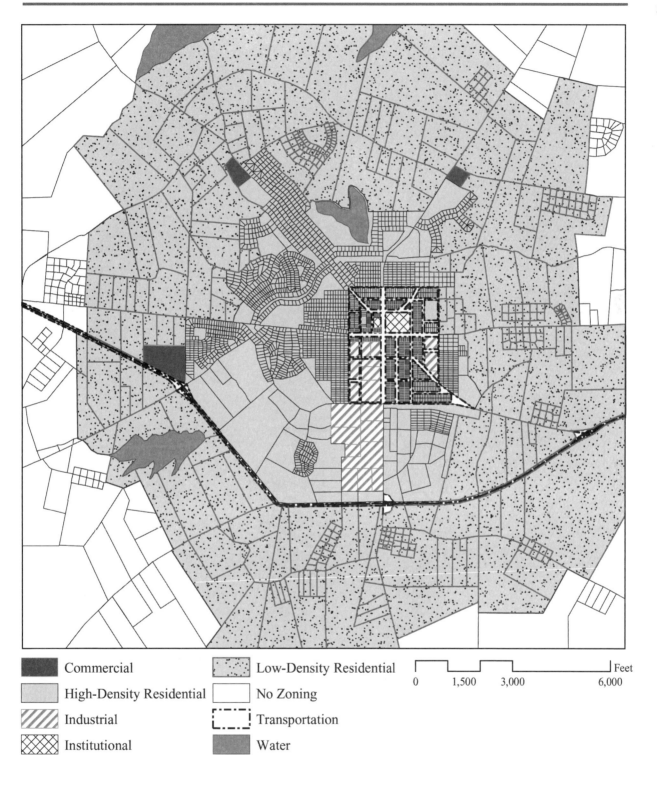

Commercial

High-Density Residential

Industrial

Institutional

Low-Density Residential

No Zoning

Transportation

Water

0   1,500   3,000   6,000   Feet

Map 18   Existing Zoning and Extraterritorial Jurisdiction Limits

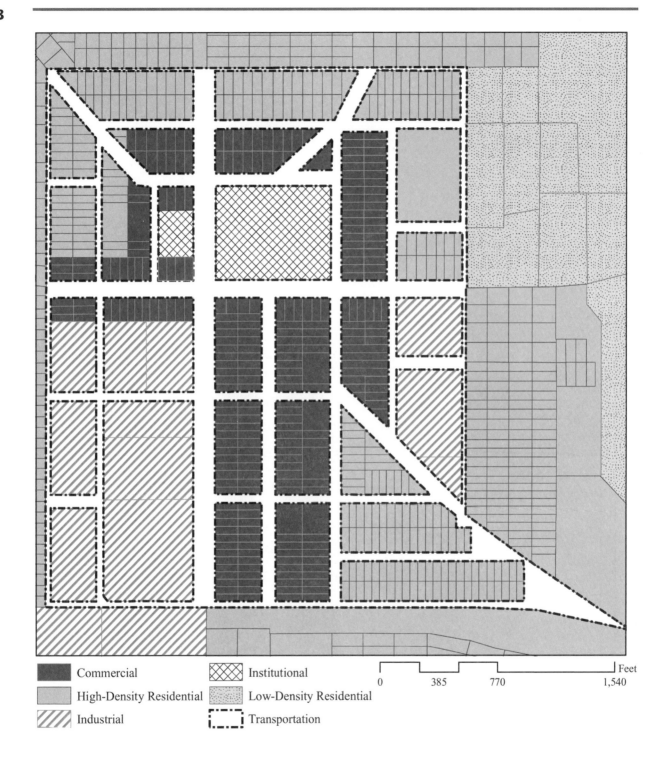

■ Commercial	⧉ Institutional		
▨ High-Density Residential	⠿ Low-Density Residential		
▨ Industrial	⌐˙⌐ Transportation		

			Feet
0	385	770	1,540

Map 19 Existing Zoning in the CBD

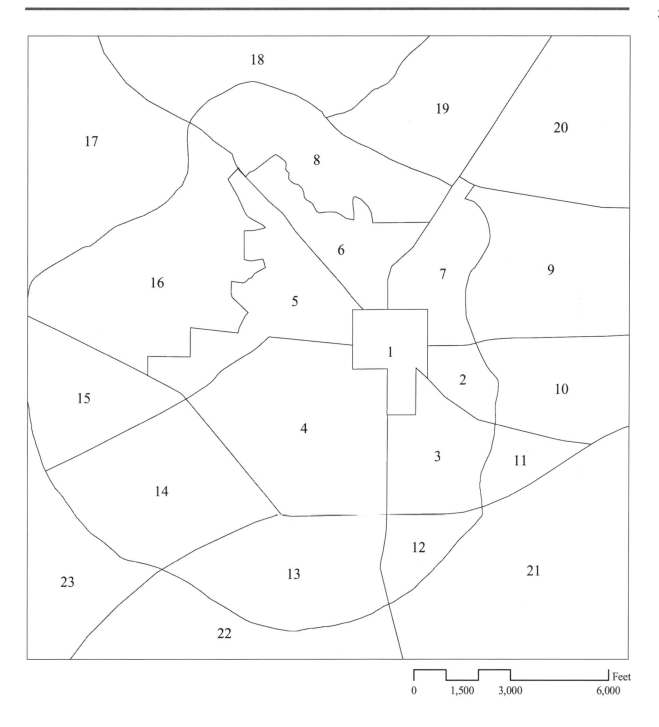

Map 20 Planning Districts

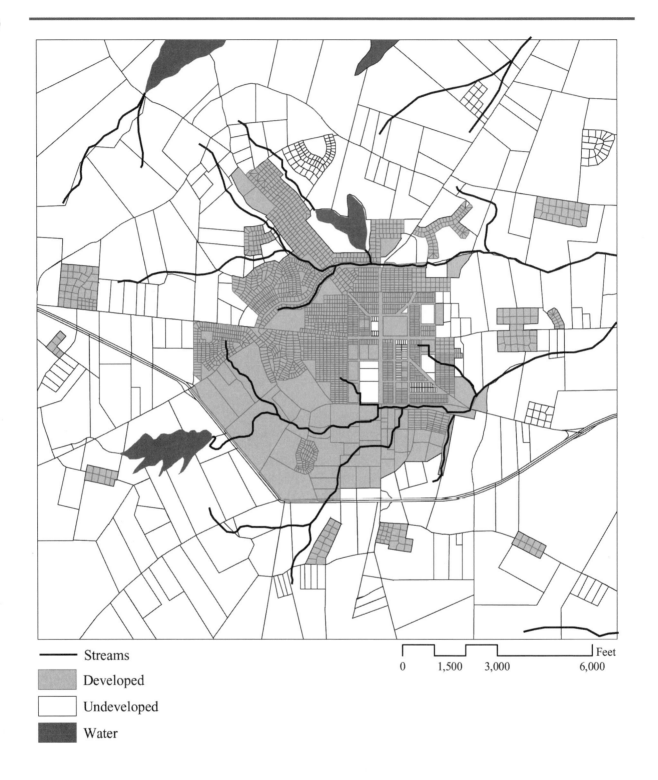

Streams

Developed

Undeveloped

Water

Map 21 Current Urban Development

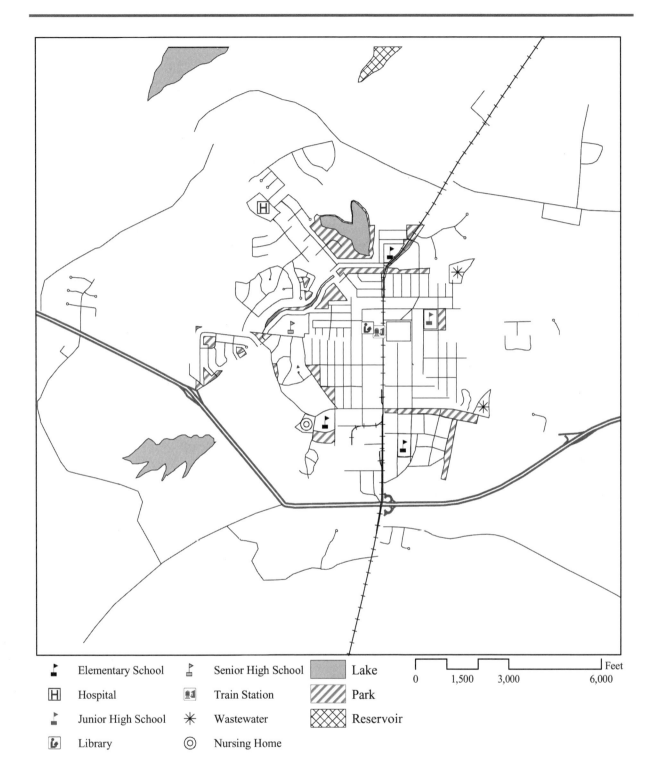

Symbol	Feature	Symbol	Feature	Symbol	Feature
⚑	Elementary School	⚑	Senior High School	▨	Lake
Ⓗ	Hospital	🏢	Train Station	▨	Park
⚑	Junior High School	✳	Wastewater	▨	Reservoir
📖	Library	◎	Nursing Home		

Scale: 0 — 1,500 — 3,000 — 6,000 Feet

Map 22   Location of Public Services

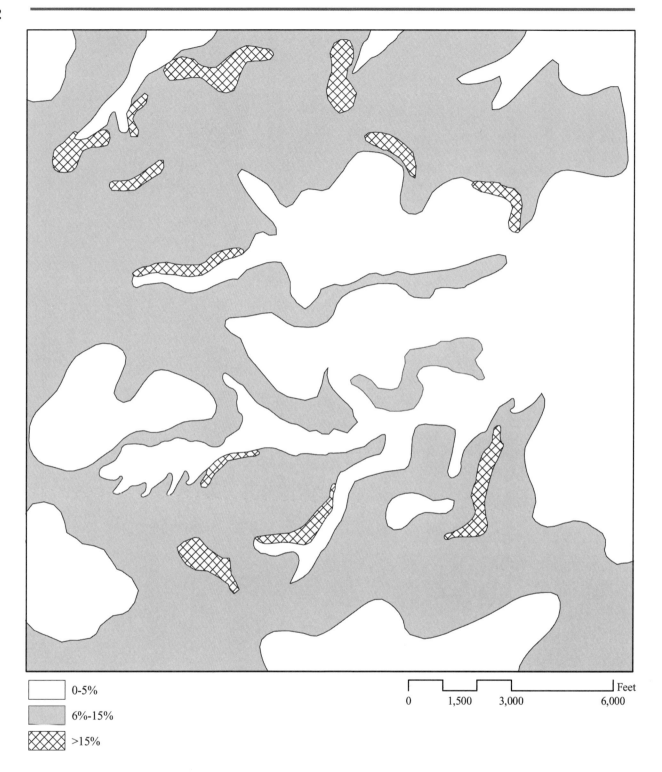

0-5%

6%-15%

>15%

0   1,500   3,000   6,000 | Feet

Map 23 Slopes

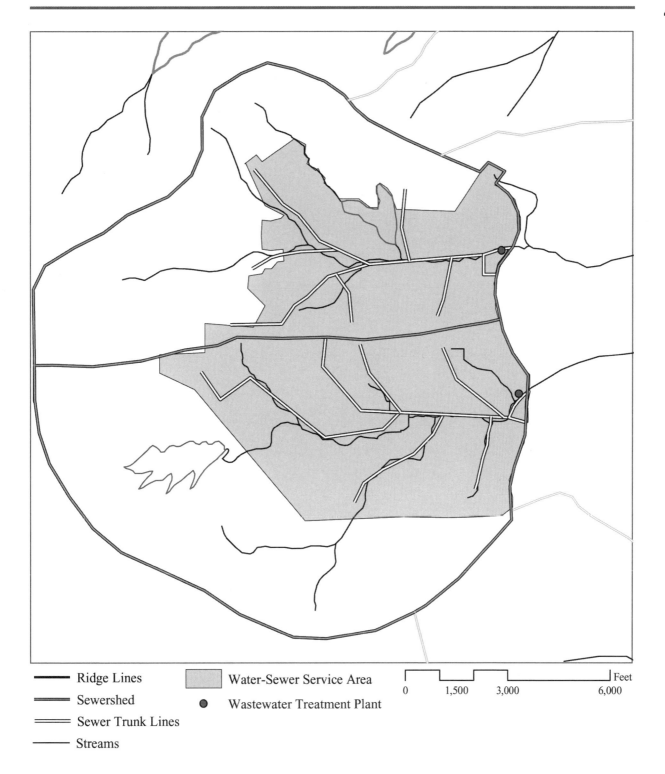

Ridge Lines

Sewershed

Sewer Trunk Lines

Streams

Water-Sewer Service Area

● Wastewater Treatment Plant

Feet

0   1,500   3,000   6,000

Map 24 Sewer Utility Factors

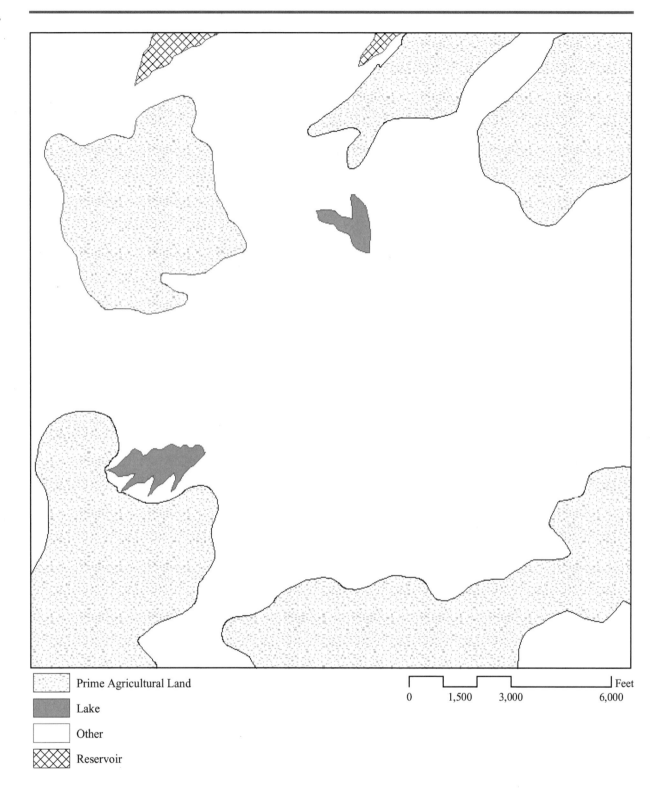

Prime Agricultural Land

Lake

Other

Reservoir

0   1,500   3,000   6,000   Feet

Map 25   Prime Agricultural Lands

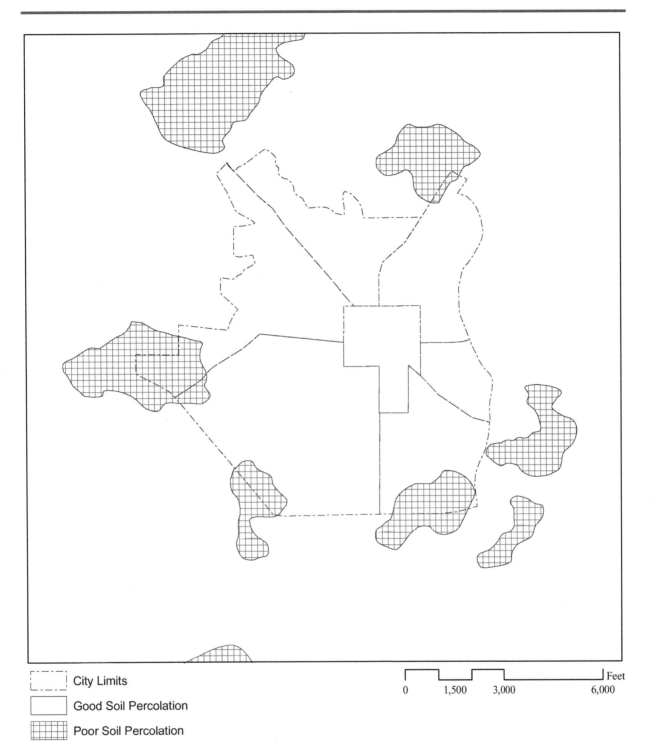

City Limits

Good Soil Percolation

Poor Soil Percolation

Feet

0   1,500   3,000   6,000

Map 26   Poor Soil Percolation

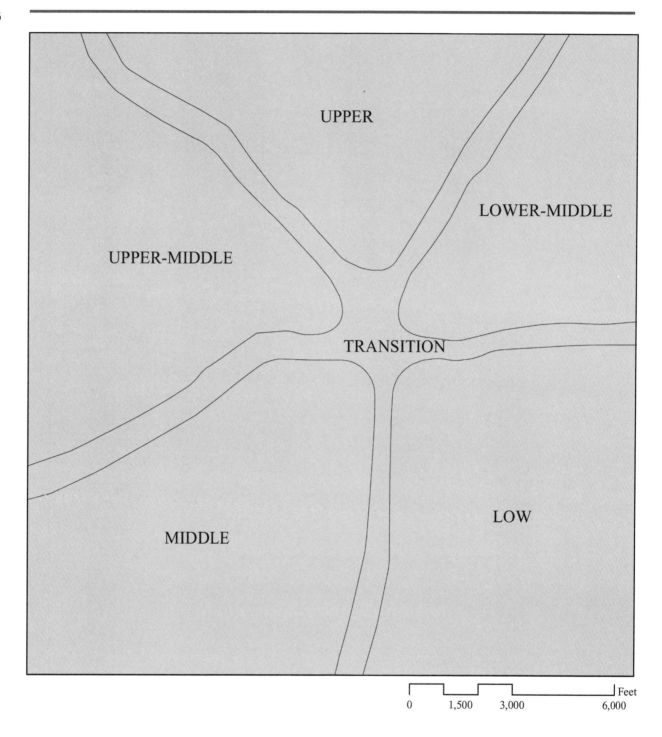

Map 27 Distribution of Socioeconomic Classes

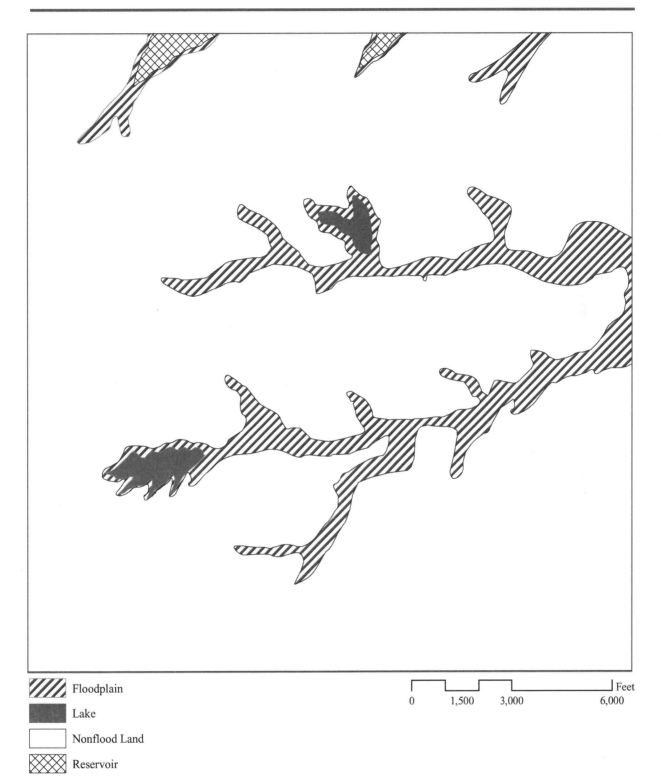

Floodplain

Lake

Nonflood Land

Reservoir

0   1,500   3,000   6,000   Feet

Map 28   100-Year Floodplains

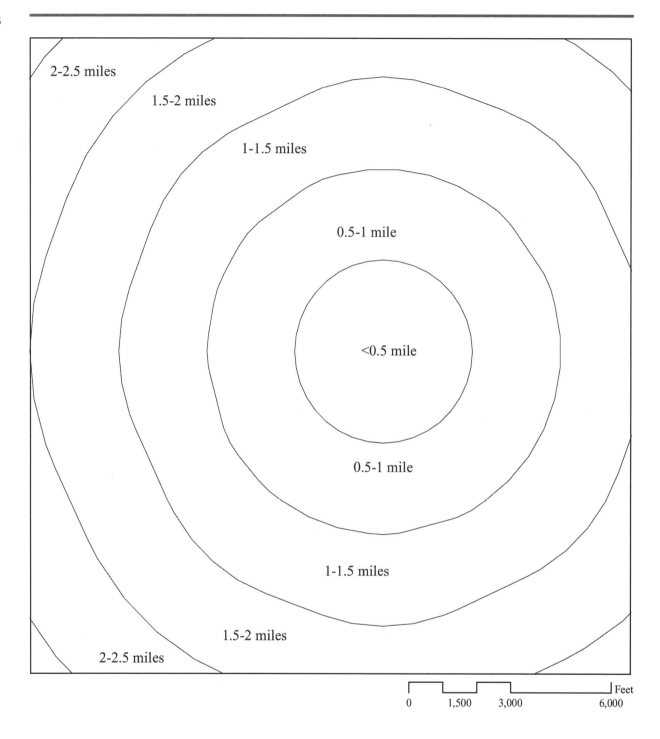

Map 29   Buffer Distances from the CBD

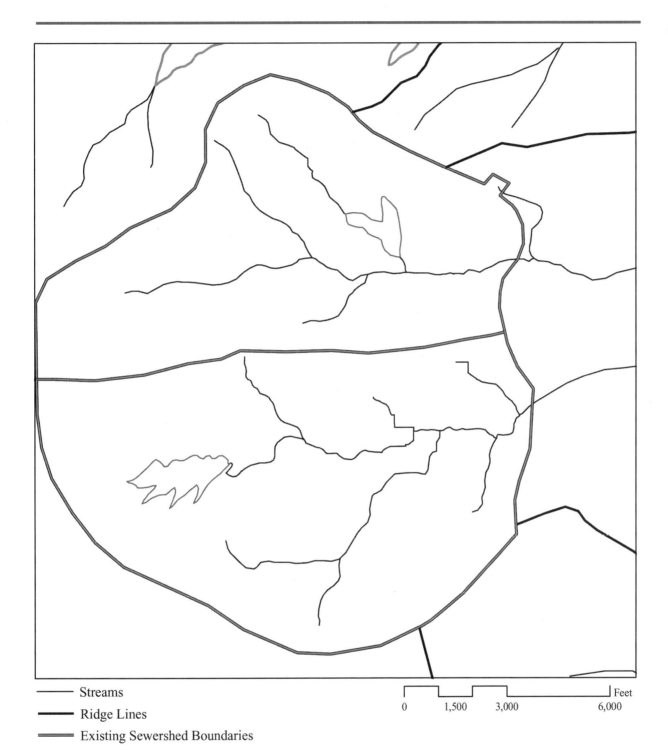

Streams

Ridge Lines

Existing Sewershed Boundaries

Feet

0   1,500   3,000   6,000

Map 30   Drainage Boundaries and Streams

PART III

Exercise Guidelines

This part of the workbook contains guidelines for each of the plan-making exercises: eight basic and nine supporting exercises. The exercises can be undertaken either as team or individual projects. However, we recommend that users work in teams of four to five people, which encourages interactive learning and more thoroughly analyzed and prepared plans. Working in teams also reflects typical land use planning practice.

Several of the exercises require the use of ArcGIS software to make maps, project future development patterns, construct land suitability analyses, allocate land uses, and balance future land use requirement against land supply.

Overview of Plan-making Exercises

The eight basic exercises constitute successive phases of the plan-making process, from initial scoping of trends and conditions through the formulation of goals and planning proposals to plan preparation, development-management program design, plan evaluation, and plan document production. They are designed as sequential activities, in which each phase builds on the results of previous phases. The end result is a completely analyzed and specified future land use plan.

The nine supporting exercises supplement the basic plan-making tasks. They guide the user through a number of technical assignments, from mapping existing conditions, through public participation meetings, suitability analysis, and both analytical and synthetic plan-making tasks. They are done in connection with basic tasks and may be revised as the user develops a clearer sense of the ramifications of early assumptions and decisions.

First we give an overview description of the complete set of basic and supporting plan-making exercises, so the user can grasp the content of, and interconnections within, the full set of exercises. (Refer to Figure 1 for a graphic overview of the exercise set.) Second, we provide detailed guidelines for completing each individual exercise.

We have placed the plan evaluation criteria in the final supporting exercise (i.e. Supporting Exercise I), but strongly advise students to take a look at them throughout the planning process to help assess how they are doing in producing the plan elements. Instructors can also incorporate them into a plan review or plan comparison exercise before the teams begin work on their Hypo City plans. They are essentially a statement of what makes a good plan. Instructors should refer to "Notes to Instructor" (Part IV of workbook) for additional advice.

Exercise 1 – Creating a "State of Community" Report

Creating a "State of Community" Report familiarizes the user with existing conditions and likely planning issues in Hypo City. It asks the user to describe and analyze the data provided in the workbook text, tables, and maps and to flesh them out in a customized version that expands on the workbook's base case data. The result is a summary description of existing and emerging conditions, planning issues, and future development scenarios in Hypo City that serves as a basis for the remainder of the plan. It applies the procedures discussed in chapters 4 through 9 in *Urban Land Use Planning, 5th edition.*

Supporting Exercise A. Computer Mapping of Existing Conditions supplements the State of Community Report with maps of significant planning features that indicate issues to be addressed in future land use planning.

Supporting Exercise B. Conducting a Community Visioning Meeting has the user conduct a participatory visioning exercise to simulate initial citizen involvement in the planning process and to broaden the planner's sense of public concerns and issues prior to undertaking the technical analyses and design steps.

Supporting Exercise C. Constructing Alternative Scenarios for Future Community Development supplements Exercise 1 with alternative land use/development scenarios for Hypo City and (if completed) the evaluation and selection of a preferred choice. It provides a foundation and starting point for the discussion of community goals, objectives, and policies, and for the preparation of the network of plans to guide future growth and development. It applies the procedures discussed in chapter 9 of *Urban Land Use Planning, 5th edition.*

Exercise 2 – Creating a Direction-setting Framework

Creating a Direction-setting Framework calls on the user to generate goals, objectives, and verbal policy statements. These are packaged with a community assessment, derived from Exercise 1, to constitute what is called a "direction-setting framework" in chapter 10 of *Urban Land Use Planning, 5th edition.*

Exercise 3 – Creating an Areawide Land Policy Plan

Creating an Areawide Land Policy plan requires the user to formulate an areawide land policy plan based on the assessments, alternative land use/development scenarios, goals, and general policies compiled in Exercises 1 and 2. The areawide land policy plan will contain both a *map* of proposed land policy districts, properly sized and reflecting development suitability and environmental vulnerability, and implementation *policies* for each district. The methodology is described in chapters 3, 10, and 11 in *Urban Land Use Planning, 5th edition.*

Supporting Exercise D.   Land Suitability Analysis provides instructions on the use of GIS technology to explore the suitability of land within the planning area for various types of uses, such as conservation or urban transition.

Supporting Exercise E.   Computerized Land Policy District Classification lets the user try out and produce maps of different land policy classification schemes with the GIS software.

Exercise 4 – Creating a Communitywide Land Use Design

Creating a Communitywide Land Use Design requires the user to develop an urban land use design, specifying the uses of all land within the future community. It can be prepared independently of the areawide land policy plan (if Exercise 3 is not done). This exercise addresses procedures and issues discussed in chapters 10, 12, and 13 of *Urban Land Use Planning, 5th edition.*

Supporting Exercise F.   Computerized Land Use Design provides general instructions for creating alternative land use design schemes with the GIS software.

Supporting Exercise G.   Land Supply and Demand Acreage by Generalized Land Use Category provides the user with a basic accounting system for balancing land supply and demand.

Exercise 5 – Creating a Small-area Plan

Creating a Small-area Plan provides some background information on how the previous exercises can be modified to focus on special areas within the community. It applies the procedures discussed in chapter 14, "Small-area Plans," in *Urban Land Use Planning, 5th edition.*

Exercise 6 – Preparing a Development-management Program

Preparing a Development-management Program requires the user to formulate a land Development-management Program to implement the land use patterns and policies of one or all of the areawide land policy plan, the communitywide land use design, and the small-area plan. The program proposes regulations, public investments, and other measures to influence the rate, amount, type, location, cost, quality, and impact of development in accordance with the policies contained in the previously formulated plan components. This exercise addresses procedures and issues discussed in chapter 15, "Development-management Plans," in *Urban Land Use Planning, 5th edition.*

Exercise 7 – Evaluating the Plan

Evaluating the Plan asks the user to evaluate the proposed final plan or perhaps to compare and evaluate two or more alternative plans. This evaluation can take the form of a technical assessment of the planning proposals, a community-based assessment, or both.

Supporting Exercise H.   Plan Review Public Hearing simulates a public hearing to illustrate how different community stakeholders might respond to plan proposals and how political fortunes could be affected by elected officials' support (or rejection) of plan alternatives.

Exercise 8 – Producing the Complete Plan

Producing the Complete Plan requires the user to compile the results of all the previous assignments into a complete future land use plan, including the State of Community Report, the direction-setting framework, the areawide land policy plan, the communitywide land use design, a small-area plan, the development-management program, and any changes resulting from the plan evaluation. This document becomes the plan of record for the community. It should be a unified report, with all necessary text, maps, tables, and graphics presented in a consistent and readable format.

Supporting Exercise I. Critique of Planning Methodology and Plan Quality Evaluation Protocol asks the user to (1) reflect on the strengths and weaknesses of the land use planning process, and (2) go through a plan quality checklist. This exercise addresses procedures discussed in chapters 3 and 10 in *Urban Land Use Planning, 5th edition.*

Customizing Hypo City

In order to enrich the planning experience, students often customize Hypo City to meet their particular interests. The number of possible variations is limited only by the user's imagination. Several examples from past student plans are provided here to illustrate some of the possibilities. It is also possible to vary other base case conditions, such as growth rate, demographic makeup, environmental constraints, land use attributes, and housing conditions. These examples are suggestive only. Many other possibilities can be formulated.

Maple Grove, Maine. This small inland community is located on the mid-southern coast of Maine. The town is anticipating a period of unprecedented growth from the rise of the tourism and real estate industries. New residents are migrating from Boston attracted by low land values and a beautiful setting. Lack of planning has led to the beginnings of sprawl, the deterioration of the central planning districts, and a lack of affordable housing. The Maple Grove planning commission has initiated this plan to curb these trends and guide development in a sustainable manner.

Chickasaw, Mississippi. The city finds itself at an important crossroads, and planners are aware that a number of social and economic forces will change the community dramatically over the next two decades. The opening of a new Mississippi State University College of Veterinary Medicine is one major factor contributing to growth. The city is embarking on creating a land use plan that will protect valuable natural and historic resources and maintain quality of life while accommodating the anticipated economic growth and infrastructure needs over the next twenty years.

Waterberry, Ohio. This midwestern city is recovering from a major flood that devastated large areas in the floodplains of the two primary water courses. Among its important planning concerns are mitigation of natural hazard impacts through a townwide redevelopment and open-space acquisition policy. It proposes designating all floodplains as community greenways and relocating existing structures outside the floodplains.

Moraine, Vermont. This New England city has a tradition of high-quality manufacturing dating from the nineteenth century, when it started producing furniture and outdoor recreation equipment. Today, its industrial base has broadened to include precision optical instrumentation and electronics. Its water supply comes from the Cold River Reservoir and the St. Lawrence Aquifer, both designated as critical conservation areas and as sending areas for the proposed transfer of development rights. One of its major public facilities needs is a new aquifer water-supply source.

Dobbs Hill, Virginia. Located adjacent to the Dobbs Hill Civil War Battlefield, this historic community has buildings dating to the mid-1880s, including the rail station, courthouse, factories, and smaller commercial and residential buildings. Two blocks on Main Street have been designated as a Virginia Heritage Area. Among its planning concerns are the protection of its battlefield and other historic sites in the face of increasing development pressures, as well as preservation of its prime farmlands, which have been in cultivation since the Revolutionary War, as part of its historic rural character.

Nootka Bay, Washington.   The CBD of this city faces Puget Sound to the east (Planning Districts 9 and 10 become part of the Sound). Its urban area is surrounded by the evergreens of the Olympic National Forest. Native Americans make up part of its population. Its economic base is evolving from timber and fishing toward corporate headquarters and research and development offices, in the wake of regionwide economic growth. Among its important planning concerns are waterfront redevelopment, including marina improvements and adaptive reuse of existing waterfront industrial structures, along with conservation of forest and bay environmental quality.

Exercise Guidelines

These guidelines are written in the form of individual exercise assignments. Although they describe the desired products, they are not entirely sufficient by themselves for completing the exercises. Users need to read the appropriate parts of *Urban Land Use Planning, 5th edition,* and other assigned reading and follow any supplementary instructions given by the instructor.

Supporting exercises are designed to contribute to the accomplishment of the basic exercises and to enrich the educational experience of the student. The supporting exercises include both technical and participatory activities. Although the plan can be prepared without undertaking the supporting exercises, we recommend that they be included wherever feasible. Students will need to know the basics of ArcGIS software for some of the exercises.

The following sections provide guidelines for completing both the basic and the supporting exercises. Each basic exercise is described first, followed by the relevant supporting exercise or exercises.

Exercise 1
Creating a "State of Community" Report

Product: A written and graphic description of existing and emerging conditions, planning issues, opportunities and challenges, future land use/development scenarios, and a vision statement for the user's customized version of Hypo City.

Your task is to briefly summarize, evaluate, and report on existing and emerging conditions and trends, opportunities, and challenges in your Hypo City and to generate a vision statement and alternative land use/ development scenarios. Three products are required: a brief written report, a graphic poster, and a brief verbal presentation of your findings and conclusions.

Your written report should be succinct and your main points clearly stated, on the assumption that busy citizens and policy makers value brief and easily read materials. The suggested limit is five pages of text, not including attached graphs, diagrams, maps, or other graphics.

Your visual presentation of key findings should be in the form of a land use planning issues poster. The poster should illustrate your main points graphically, in the form of annotated maps and bulleted text suitable for a public meeting or for public viewing on a bulletin board. The suggested poster size is 24 by 36 inches (though this can be varied). The materials on the poster should be easily readable from a distance of 10 feet.

Your verbal presentation should be brief, as though you were addressing a community meeting of concerned citizens (see Cogan 1992). The presentation should use your poster as a visual aid. The suggested time limit is five minutes.

The following provides some guidance on how to proceed with generating the products listed above. See chapters 4 and 9 of *Urban Land Use Planning, 5th edition,* for more details and techniques that can be used. Suggested steps include:

1. Summarize and evaluate existing and emerging conditions and planning issues in your Hypo City

The report should identify existing and emerging conditions and major problems relating to land development and redevelopment, physical deterioration, and the location of land uses with respect to each other, to environmental factors, and to community facilities and their future expansion. It should summarize the population and economic projections provided in this workbook and convert them to first-cut space requirements. (Keep space requirement estimating procedures very simple, however. For example, you might simply multiply existing acres of developed land by a factor equal to population and employment growth ratios. There is opportunity for exploration of more detailed space requirements in later exercises.)

Issue identification uses planning intelligence to locate matters in dispute, unresolved problems, or points of debate or controversies (e.g., fragmentation of environmental resources, disconnect between land use and transportation, failing downtowns, lack of affordable housing options, forecasted rapid population growth or decline, and changing demographics). These issues help establish evaluation criteria for land use/ development scenarios and for the direction-setting framework. Graphics that show areas that are developable, not developable, developed, and perceived areas of concern are useful.

Your starting point is the base case information provided in Part II in this workbook. In addition, you can name the town, give it a special personality, place it in any state of the nation, or put it in a particular environmental setting, such as a coastline, for example. With your instructor's permission, you may also change some of the information or add factors to make the exercise more suitable for exploring particular issues, such as environmental protection or economic development issues. In any case, do not simply repeat what is in the text, tables, and maps in the workbook; interpret it.

As another optional element, you may include maps that show locations of existing or future issues to be addressed in policy and plans; see Supporting Exercise A. Also, see the illustrative poster in Figure 2 for an example of a visual aid that pulls together a number of key issues.

2. Generate a vision statement

A vision statement can be generated based on planning intelligence gathered from the previous step. The statement should at least address questions such as: Where and how shall we develop? and How shall we grow? This can be accomplished via meetings and forums that enable community participation. Supporting Exercise B lays out a format for a community visioning meeting and lists various participation techniques that can be used.

3. Construct alternative scenarios for future community development

Scenario construction in this case deals with conceiving alternative land use/development patterns to achieve the community vision. Planning intelligence helps to shape potential futures and to establish parameters and desirable directions for development. For example, land capability intelligence about the potential for development and provision of infrastructure can suggest desirable directions for future growth and ensure that the preferred scenario (if selected) is factually grounded.

This exercise should be viewed as a starting point and foundation for selecting a preferred land development scenario; for the discussion of community goals, objectives, and policies; and for the preparation of the network of plans to guide future growth and development. The report should summarize various development scenarios considered and (if applicable) reasons supporting a preferred scenario. Maps or sketches can show, for example, preferred locations to accommodate mixed-use development. Supporting Exercise C provides guidance on how land use/development scenarios can be generated through a participatory process.

The process is usually carried out over a series of workshops with some work and GIS-based analyses (e.g., the potential impact of a particular land use scheme on natural resources) completed outside the workshop setting and then presented to participants at follow-up workshops. The process also assumes that scenarios can be modified when participants are shown outcomes of technical analyses. Overall, scenarios should be subjected to rigorous testing, both analytically and in the public arena.

GIS-based planning support systems such as What If (Klosterman 2001) and INDEX (Allen 2001) are increasingly used in planning practice to automate the entire process of exploring and evaluating alternative community-development scenarios. For example, Paint the Town (part of the INDEX suite of products) allows users to "paint" land uses and preferred growth scenarios on the fly during public meetings, thereby capturing stakeholder spatial inputs. Students who have access to planning support systems may wish to use its functionality to complete this task.

Suggested Reading

1. Allen, Elliot. 2001. INDEX: Software for community indicators. In *Planning support systems: Integrating geographic information systems, models and visualization tools,* Richard K. Brail and Richard E. Klosterman, eds., 229–61. Redlands, Calif.: ESRI Press.

2. Berke, Philip R., David R. Godschalk, Edward J. Kaiser, with Daniel A. Rodriguez. 2006. *Urban land use planning,* 5th ed. (ch. 4, Planning support systems; ch. 5, Population and economy; ch. 6, Environmental systems; ch. 7, Land use systems; ch. 8, Transportation and infrastructure systems; ch. 9, State of community report). Urbana: University of Illinois Press.

3. Cogan, E. 1992. *Successful public meetings: A practical guide for managers in government.* (ch. 5, Making effective presentations; ch. 6, Using audiovisuals). San Francisco: Jossey-Bass.

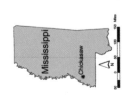

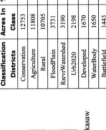

Figure 2. Illustrative Poster

4. Dieber, M., and E. Allen. 210 cities paint their future with GIS. *ESRI ArcNews* (Winter 2003/2004). http://www.esri.com/ news/arcnews/winter0304articles/210-cities.html.

5. INDEX Web site. http://www.crit.com.

6. Klosterman, Richard. 2001. The what if planning support system. In *Planning support systems: Integrating geographic information systems, models, and visualization tools,* Richard K. Brail and Richard E. Klosterman, eds., 263–84. Redlands, Calif.: ESRI Press.

Supporting Exercise A
Computer Mapping of Existing Conditions

Product: Maps of existing conditions in Hypo City

In this exercise you will create maps of Hypo City township and city planning areas as part of a poster.

This exercise complements Exercise 1, in which you are required to evaluate and summarize existing conditions in Hypo City. It allows you to quickly and efficiently visualize, combine, and display the existing environmental and infrastructure conditions/constraints (such as roads, sewer lines, and treatment plants), natural resources, current land use and zoning, barriers to development, and location of developed areas. This is done by opening the map files (from the workbook CD) in ESRI ArcGIS software where you can work with the maps and the associated databases. You must have access to and knowledge of basic operating procedures in ArcGIS to carry out this exercise.

Tables 10 and 11 (in Part II) contain the name and description of each map file (at the township and city planning area scales, respectively). The township-level files listed in Table 10 are stored in the Township directory created by the installation program. The city planning area files listed in Table 11 are stored in the HypoCity directory created by the installation program. The section "Maps of Existing Conditions" in Part II of this workbook should also be referenced for a more detailed description of the maps.

Departments with in-house GIS lab facilities may wish to create a folder/directory for each planning team to keep the original data intact.

Some ArcGIS terminology:

- Layer: a collection of similar geographic features (such as roads, forests, or planning districts) in a particular area or place referenced together for display on a map. A layer references geographic data stored in a data source (such as a coverage) and defines how to display it (ArcGIS Help Glossary).

- Data Frame: a frame on the map that displays layers occupying the same geographic area (ArcGIS Help Glossary).

- Data View: an all-purpose view in ArcMap and ArcReader for exploring, displaying, and querying geographic data.

- Layout View: the view for laying out your map in ArcMap and ArcReader. Shows the virtual page upon which you place and arrange geographic data and map elements (such as titles, legends, and scale bars) for printing.

- Table of Contents: lists all the data frames and layers on the map and shows what features the symbols in each layer represents.

- Map Documents: contain file paths to where data files are actually stored on your computer. An ArcMap document only saves these pathways, not the data sets themselves. Map documents are saved with a special file name extension (*.mxd*).

- ArcGIS functions: menus are shown in bold and italic with the first letter underlined (e.g., ***P*rint**). Buttons that you click with your mouse to perform an action (e.g., ***Apply*** and ***OK***) or command lines that prompt you for input (e.g., ***Layer Name)*** are shown in bold and italic. File names (e.g., *landclas.shp*) or fields in tables (e.g., *ACRES, LUDESIGN*) are shown in italic.

Overview of Exercise

In this exercise, you will manipulate the Hypo City map files with ArcGIS. First launch ArcMap and select *A new empty map*. This will create a new map document for which you can then begin to add layers to the data frame in order to create your own maps of existing conditions. The basic steps are:

1. Begin the mapping session by opening ArcMap.
2. Add layers and change the drawing order.
3. Rename layers to correspond to your map legend titles.
4. Define map units to create proper scale.
5. Create your desired map patterns and colors.
6. Add data frames.
7. Create map layouts and add legends, scale bars, north arrow, and titles to your map.
8. Add and symbolize the legend.
9. Print and plot your maps.
10. Save your work before exiting.

ArcGIS Instructions

Step 1: Begin the mapping session by opening ArcMap

- Install the GIS files (from the accompanying CD) onto your hard drive. Instructions are provided in the section "Installation" in Part I of the workbook.
- Open ArcMap and select *A new empty map* when prompted.
- Use the *Add Data* button to add the desired layers to the data frame by navigating to the drive and directory to which the ArcGIS shape files were copied. If you copied your GIS files to C:\Hypocity, then the files listed in Table 10 will be stored in the C:\HypoCity\Township directory and the files listed in Table 11 will be stored in the C:\HypoCity\HypoCity directory.

Step 2: Add layers and change the drawing order

In ArcGIS, you can control which layers are displayed in your data frame by simply turning them on or off, using the box located next to the layer's name in the table of contents. The order in which layers are drawn in the table of contents is important since the layer at the top of the table of contents is drawn on top of those below it. Layers that form the background to your data frame should therefore be at the bottom of the list.

- Use your mouse to click on the name of the layer and drag it up or down to change the order in the table of contents.
- To make a layer active, left click on the layer name in the table of contents (the layer name should become highlighted in blue). A layer must be active in order for changes to be made to that layer.

Step 3: Rename layers to correspond to your map legend titles

A layer is added to a data frame with the corresponding map file names. You will want to rename the layer to reflect how you want it to appear in your map legend. To rename the layer (in the table of contents):

- Right click on the layer name and select *Properties* from the menu.
- Click on the *General* tab and change the layer name in the "layer name" box. You can also change the layer name by clicking twice on the layer name in the table of contents. A cursor will appear and the layer name will be highlighted. Simply type in the new layer name.

Step 4: Define map units to create proper scale

In order to use the scale bar in your layout, you must define the map units. To do this, select **Data Frame Properties** from the **View** menu. Click on the **General** tab and set the *Map Units* to *inches* (since this is the unit of the Hypo City digital maps). Once this is predefined, the scale bar can be set to convert to and display other map units (e.g., feet or miles).

Step 5: Create your desired map patterns and colors

To change the default patterns and colors that ArcMap selects, double click on the symbol that appears below the layer name in the table of contents to open the symbol selector. The symbol selector contains either fill, point, or line palettes depending on the type of layer. For example, if you have a shapefile of streets (which is a line file), the symbol selector will provide options to change line styles and colors.

Step 6: Add Data Frames

In ArcMap, you can have several data frames in one map document at a time. This helps with organizing layers. To add a new data frame, select **Data frame** from the **Insert** menu. A new empty data frame will be added to your table of contents. However, in data view you can only see the data frame that is currently active. To activate a data frame, right click on the data frame name (by default, the first data frame is named "layers") and select **Activate** from the menu. To change the data frame name, right click on the data frame name, select properties from the drop-down list, click on the general tab, and change the name.

Step 7: Create map layouts and add legends, scale bars, north arrow, and titles to your map

A map layout must be created before printing. In order to create a printable map, you must switch from data view to layout view. In the layout view, you can add or view map elements such as the scale bar, north arrow, and legend.

Switch to layout view:

- From the **View** menu, select **Layout view**. The main window should now display your data frame(s) on a virtual page.
- Use the **Insert** menu to add the scale bar, neatline, titles, text, and other map elements.

Insert map elements:

Each element on your layout is embedded in a frame (i.e., data frame, legend frame, scale bar frame, north arrow frame, chart frame, table frame, and picture frame). Once the layout is created, you can snap and align layout elements; move, resize, and reorder frames and elements; draw graphics and add text; import other graphics; and export the layout to other image formats. You can still work with your map layers, view attributes, and query data in layout view; however, functionality is limited. It is usually best to work in data view until you are ready to create your map layout.

Draw tools:

To add other graphics (such as lines and circles), make sure the Draw toolbar is visible by selecting **View, Toolbars, Draw**. The Draw toolbar features graphic tools similar to most graphic programs. For example, you can create a circle around a specific area of your map using the circle tool in the Draw toolbar. You may also adjust the color and fill pattern of the circle using features on the Draw toolbar.

Step 8: Add and symbolize the legend

Select **Legend** from the **Insert** menu. The Legend Wizard will appear. On the left side is a list of layers and on the right side is a list of items that will appear in your legend. By default, the software shows all layers in your legend. If you do not want to include all layers in your legend, highlight the layer name and click the left arrow. This will remove the layer and it will not appear in the legend. You can also select how many columns you want your legend to have from the drop-down menu in the window. When finished, click **Next**. The following menus allow you to select font style; font size; legend title, frame, and background; the size and shape of your symbol patches; and spacing options. Click **Next** until the **Finish** button. The legend will appear in your layout view and can be moved around like an object. Changes to layer names will automatically be updated in the legend.

Step 9: Print and plot your maps

Page Setup:

From the **_File_** menu, select **_Page and Print Setup_** to choose the size and orientation of the final output (i.e., letter, tabloid, D-size plot) and any margins that may be required. The D-size plot (24 inches by 36 inches) is the suggested poster size for Exercise 1.

Print:

Use the **Print** button or select **_Print_** from the **_File_** menu and specify the name of the layout to print and the name of the printer/plotter to be used.

The layout can also be exported to other image formats such as a Jpeg (.jpg) image file, a PDF (.pdf), or an Enhanced meta file (.Emf) for easy printing and transferability.

Step 10: Save your work before exiting

From the **_File_** menu, choose **_Save As_**. In the dialog box that appears, specify a name and location for the new project file and press **Save**.

To use this map document file the next time you open ArcGIS, you will need to select **_Open an Existing Map_** when opening ArcGIS or you will need to select **_Open_** from the **_File_** menu and navigate to your map document.

Suggested Reading

1. Berke, Philip R., David R. Godschalk, Edward J. Kaiser, with Daniel A. Rodriguez. 2006. _Urban land use planning_, 5th ed. (ch. 4, Planning support systems; ch. 9, State of community report). Urbana: University of Illinois Press.
2. ESRI. 2001. _Getting to know ArcGIS Desktop._ Redlands, Calif.: ESRI Press.
3. Tufte, E. R. 1990. _Envisioning information._ Cheshire, Conn.: Graphics Press.

Supporting Exercise B
Conducting a Community Visioning Meeting

Product: A participatory meeting to identify future planning issues.

Prepare and conduct a community visioning meeting to identify future planning issues and an overall vision through a participatory process. The purpose of this exercise is to simulate citizen feedback on the planning team's initial interpretation of planning information/data and issues of concern for input into the State of Community Report. In order to give a sense of the nature of the participation process, one team is selected to conduct the meeting while other students act as community participants responding to the presentation. The goal is to design a collaborative planning process aimed at envisioning and developing a sustainable community.

The team conducting the exercise selects the technique to be used, runs the meeting, and prepares a brief report on the outcome. The following participation techniques are most useful for small group meetings of selected participants in face-to-face settings (see details in chapter 9 of _Urban Land Use Planning, 5th edition_).

- Charrettes (Segedy and Johnson nd), which bring together citizens and design professionals to solve problems and generate alternative solutions (usually in the form of sketches)

- Silent reflection and follow-up discussion, as in the nominal group technique (Cogan 1992; Delbecq, Van de Ven, and Gustafson 1975)
- Brainstorming and follow-up discussions to generate creative ideas with small groups (Cogan 1992; Sanoff 2000)
- Focus groups led by moderators through discussions of issues and goals (Krueger 1988)
- The snow card display and voting technique (Bryson and Crosby 1992)

To present the necessary background information, the team conducting the meeting can use its existing and emerging issues poster along with a brief verbal summary. It can hand out an information outline and a list of questions to consider, such as: What effects will the projected population growth have on community character? Where should new commercial and industrial uses be located? How will future development affect the natural environment? Where and how shall we grow?

The challenge will be to organize and manage the session so that discussion is focused on future land use issues and goals (versus issues that cannot be dealt with in a land use plan), and so that participants' concerns are voiced and considered. The conducting team should provide moderators for the group discussions and expressions of priorities and recorders to capture participant statements.

A suggested meeting format is:

• Participant introductions	10 minutes
• Introduction of process and planning issues (including a brief review of the State of Community Report)	10 minutes
• Moderated small-group discussions	30 minutes
• Priority expression by participants	20 minutes
• Discussion of group issues and priorities	15 minutes

Following the meeting, the team conducting the exercise should compile a brief written listing of the concerns, goals, and priorities expressed by the participants. This should be circulated to all those taking part as a record of initial community response.

Planners may also choose to collect opinions or responses to planning issues from larger numbers of participants in remote settings. Surveys (Cohen 2000; Dillman 1999) and Delphi techniques (Delbecq, Van de Ven, and Gustafson 1975) are most commonly used. Web sites have become a popular medium for eliciting responses and sharing other information.

Suggested Reading

1. Berke, Philip R., David R. Godschalk, Edward J. Kaiser, with Daniel A. Rodriguez. 2006. *Urban land use planning,* 5th ed. (ch. 9, State of community report). Urbana: University of Illinois Press.
2. Bryson, J. M., and B. C. Crosby. 1992. *Leadership for the common good.* San Francisco: Jossey-Bass.
3. Cogan, Elaine. 1992. *Successful public meetings: A practical guide for managers in government.* San Francisco: Jossey-Bass.
4. Cohen, Jonathan. 2000. *Communication and design with the Internet: A guide for architects, planners, and building professionals.* New York: Norton.
5. Delbecq, A. L., A. H. Van de Ven, and D. H. Gustafson. 1975. *Group techniques for program planning.* Glenview, Ill: Scott, Foresman.
6. Dillman, Don. 1999. *Mail and Internet surveys: The tailored design method,* 2nd ed. New York: John Wiley.
7. Krueger, R. A. 1988. *Focus groups: A practical guide for applied research.* Newbury Park, Calif.: Sage.
8. Sanoff, Henry. 2000. *Community participation methods in design and planning.* New York: John Wiley.
9. Segedy, James A., and Bradley E. Johnson. Nd. *The neighborhood charrette handbook.* Louisville, Ky.: University of Louisville. www.louisville.edu/org/sun/planning/char.html.

Supporting Exercise C
Constructing Alternative Scenarios for Future Community Development

Product: a visual representation of land use/development scenarios generated by citizens and local interest groups.

Scenarios are most applicable in situations where significant change is likely, outcomes are not obvious, and the time frame is medium to long term (10- to 20-plus years). Scenarios can also be used in the planning process to begin to respond to questions such as: Where and how shall we grow? Where should new commercial and industrial uses be located? What areas should be developed at higher densities? What open space and agricultural areas should be preserved?

The purpose of this exercise is to develop a map-based vision of future development in Hypo City through a participatory process. A workshop or charrette format is suggested (see Supporting Exercise B for a list of participation techniques). The workshop tasks outlined below are based on the process used by the Tompkins County Planning Department (TCPD) and the Ithaca-Tompkins County Transportation Council (ITCTC) as part of their Vital Communities Initiative (TCPD and ITCTC 2001).

Suggested preworkshop tasks

- Invite participants from a wide range of agencies and local interest groups including local planning, neighborhood quality, land development, environment, agriculture, economic development, education, youth, recreation, youth, transportation, and infrastructure

- Provide participants with background material and information related to workshop goals; strategic intelligence concerning the community's economy and population, environment, land use, transportation and infrastructure systems, and emerging opportunities and threats (see outcomes from supporting exercises A and B)

Suggested workshop format

- Participant introductions   10 minutes
- Review of workshop goals (e.g., whether to have participants construct alternative scenarios or have a follow-up session to have them assess a range of alternative strategies and voice their preferences)   10 minutes
- Review background materials and assign groups/teams.   10 minutes
- Groups discuss principles and indicators to be used to guide mapping (i.e., what aspects of life do they value and feel are important to preserve or improve upon in the future).   20 minutes
- Outline at least two alternative scenarios (e.g., one based on standard suburban development and one based on more compact, walkable patterns). Participants can also choose to construct the scenarios for a series of related indicators (e.g., traffic congestion, density, quality of life).   25 minutes
- Color a base map (on a transparent sheet) to indicate preferred locations for future development. The process assumes that scenarios can be modified when participants are shown outcomes of technical analyses.   45 minutes

Note: Workshop organizers should select group members so that there is a mix of interests and provide each group with hard copies of Hypo City maps. A moderator/recorder should also be assigned to each group. His or her role is to keep the group focused on task, to ensure that the group is basing scenarios on population and economic growth projections and needs, to elicit the principles and criteria that are being used to draw the map(s), and to record in detail the reasoning behind the development of the map.

Postworkshop tasks (if necessary)

Planning team members should use the input from the workshop to analyze alternatives (i.e., the likely impacts of each alternative scenario), to understand land capability and suitability (see Supporting Exercise D), and to assess the feasibility for implementation. The analysis and results should be presented at a follow-up workshop as background for refining scenarios or selecting a preferred development scenario. Alternatively, students who have access to What If and INDEX may wish to integrate these GIS-based planning support systems so that tasks are completed on the fly.

Suggested Readings:

1. Allen, Elliot. 2001. INDEX: Software for community indicators. In *Planning support systems: Integrating geographic information systems, models and visualization tools*, Richard K. Brail and Richard E. Klosterman, eds., 229–61. Redlands, Calif.: ESRI Press.

2. Berke, Philip R., David R. Godschalk, Edward J. Kaiser, with Daniel A. Rodriguez. 2006. *Urban land use planning*, 5th ed. (ch. 4, Planning support systems; ch. 9, State of community report). Urbana: University of Illinois Press.

3. Dieber, M., and E. Allen. 210 Cities paint their future with GIS. *ESRI ArcNews* (Winter 2003/2004). http://www.esri.com/news/arcnews/winter0304articles/210-cities.html

4. INDEX website: http://www.crit.com

5. Klosterman, Richard. 2001. The What If Planning Support System. In *Planning support systems: Integrating geographic information systems, models and visualization tools*, Richard K. Brail and Richard E. Klosterman, eds., 263–84. Redlands, Calif.: ESRI Press.

6. TCPD and ITCTC. 2001. Vital communities workshop report, 2000–2001. http://www.tompkins-co.org/planning/vci/execreport.html

7. What-If website: http://www.what-if-pss.com/

Exercise 2
Creating a Direction-setting Framework

Product: A direction-setting framework statement to include an analysis of existing and emerging conditions (from Exercise 1) and a set of proposed land use goals and objectives and coordinated policies to implement the scenario that best achieves the vision.

Your task is to write a proposed direction-setting framework of community *goals* (ultimate ends being pursued), associated *objectives* (intermediate, specific, measurable, achievable accomplishments that constitute milestones toward a goal), and implementation *policies* (statement of actions or requirements judged to be necessary to achieve planning goals and objectives). Linkages between goals, objectives, and policy statements should be clear. Connections of policies to existing and emerging conditions and preferred scenarios and visions (Exercise 1) should also be logical and clear. (See illustrative example of a goals/objectives/policies statement below.)

Goal 1: A compact and contiguous urban landscape that enhances the city's livability.

> **Objective 1.1:** By 2025, achieve an average density of ten dwelling units per acre.
>
> > Policy 1.1.1: Amend the development ordinance to establish minimum density requirements for all new large-scale subdivision proposals.
>
> **Objective 1.2:** By 2025, achieve a design mix of linked housing and work areas in 50 percent of new development proposals.
>
> > **Policy 1.2.1:** Amend the development ordinance to create mixed-use districts with incentives for including both residential and employment uses within all new large-scale development project proposals.
>
> **Objective 1.3:** By 2025, increase pedestrian and cycling travel from the current 5 percent of journey-to-work trips to 10 percent.
>
> > **Policy 1.3.1:** Designate and construct a safe and continuous bicycle and pedestrian network that connects all residential and employment areas.
> >
> > **Policy 1.3.2:** Establish a transportation management program to provide employee incentives for walking and cycling to work.

Goal 2: Public facilities and services that efficiently serve new development.

> **Objective 2.1:** By 2025, bring average public costs of services per new household to regional averages.
>
> > **Policy 2.1.1:** Coordinate public and private development by establishing an "adequate facilities" requirement in development regulations and in the capital improvements plan.
> >
> > **Policy 2.1.2:** Enhance the efficiency of service provision by promoting the use of cluster development through incentives in the development ordinance.
> >
> > **Policy 2.1.3:** Establish a sliding-scale development-impact fee system that reflects true costs and variability in costs of providing services.

Specific milestones and standards should be formulated whenever possible. For example, if there is a policy to avoid new development in the floodplain, the standard might specify the fifty-year floodplain as indicated on a particular map.

The suggested target limit for the text is four pages for the policy framework, not including supporting maps, tables, and graphics. It should be organized and presented to facilitate understanding of citizens and policy makers, your primary audience. The material need not be structured in the same way as the example above, as long as it communicates effectively. The essence of the policy framework is to state the important values, measurable indicators, and policy directions for Hypo City.

This exercise may include a simulated public hearing on community problems and aspirations to discover potential citizen and stakeholder group reactions to your policy framework proposals and/or to generate community proposals for goals, objectives, and policies. A slightly modified version of Supporting Exercise B can be used as a simple approach to such a hearing.

Suggested Reading

1. Berke, Philip R., David R. Godschalk, Edward J. Kaiser, with Daniel A. Rodriguez. 2006. *Urban land use planning,* 5th ed. (ch. 3, What makes a good plan? ch. 10, The plan-making process). Urbana: University of Illinois Press.

Exercise 3
Creating an Areawide Land Policy Plan

Product: An areawide land policy plan for Hypo Township to include a map of proposed land policy districts, a table showing the number of acres in each land policy district, a list of policies for each classification district, and a brief explanation of the plan.

The areawide land policy plan lays out broad areas for urban development, urban transition, conservation, and rural or generally where development is to be encouraged (the developed and urban transition areas) and where it is to be limited (the water-supply watershed and conservation areas). It is a mapped representation and displays the community's policy toward the location and timing of future growth and infrastructure provision (see Figure 3). The alternative development scenarios (if completed as part of Supporting Exercise C) should be used as a starting point for this exercise.

The township (the larger area shown on Maps 1 through 14, which contains the Hypo City planning area as well as considerable rural land around it where urban growth pressures can be expected in the future) is the context for areawide land policy planning. This broader-scale plan is a common approach for counties and regions attempting to map general policies for land development and conservation, rather than to specify the exact land use for each land parcel.

The following classification system and suggested color code is recommended for the areawide land policy plan map:

Land Policy District	Map Color
Developed (existing)	Solid rust
Urban transition (by 2025)	Hatched rust
Rural	Light green
Water-supply watershed	Hatched darker green
Conservation	Solid darker green

The "developed" policy district should not be the same as the existing developed areas (Maps 13 and 21 for the township and city planning area, respectively); instead, it should be consciously delineated as the area in which you will focus infill and related policies. It should not include the scattered developed areas outside the city limits.

You may also include other land policy districts—for example, you might add an agricultural district separate from the rural district or a redevelopment district within the developed district. You may also divide the urban transition district into two sections, one where development will be encouraged through infrastructure scheduling for the next ten years and one for the following ten years (see Figures 11-1 and 11-2 in *Urban Land Use Planning, 5th edition*)

Along with the policy district boundaries, the map should identify existing and proposed major roads, water reservoirs and water-supply watershed boundaries, sewage treatment plants, rivers and streams, and significant environmental features to be conserved (e.g., wetlands or historic neighborhoods).

A brief text, with a suggested limit of two pages, should accompany the mapped areawide land policy plan to explain what it achieves and how. The text should include a table summarizing the number of acres and percentages of land in each policy district.

The areawide land policy plan must be designed to accommodate the projected growth of your community. So you must assign gross density policies (dwellings per acre for development occurring in the district) to the various districts. Ensure that you have classified sufficient land for future development at these densities. See Figure 4 for a suggested format.

There should be a list or table of suggested policies to promote each category in the areawide land policy plan. For example, for the transition districts, there might be a policy to promote water and sewer extensions into that area while withholding it from the rural policy districts. These policies need be described only briefly at this stage. These policies become a partial basis for the development-management plan, which will develop the policies in more detail as part of an overall growth-management strategy.

The plan should be consistent with your direction-setting framework goals and policies, assumptions, and the existing and emerging conditions that were determined in the preceding exercises. The plan should be sensitive to environmental conditions such as soils, water-supply watershed, critical environmental areas, and fertile land. It should reflect the coordination of private development with public infrastructure such as roads, water and sewer lines, treatment plants, and other growth shapers. The plan should be "reasonable," given trends, technology, projected levels of demand, environmental and infrastructure constraints, and community preferences, but at the same time it should not be a mere "projection" of past trends.

Remember that you are delineating proposed policy districts, not existing conditions. Therefore, already-developed subdivisions located in what you propose to be a rural district or a conservation district or even an urban transition district should *not* be shown as little islands of "developed" districts.

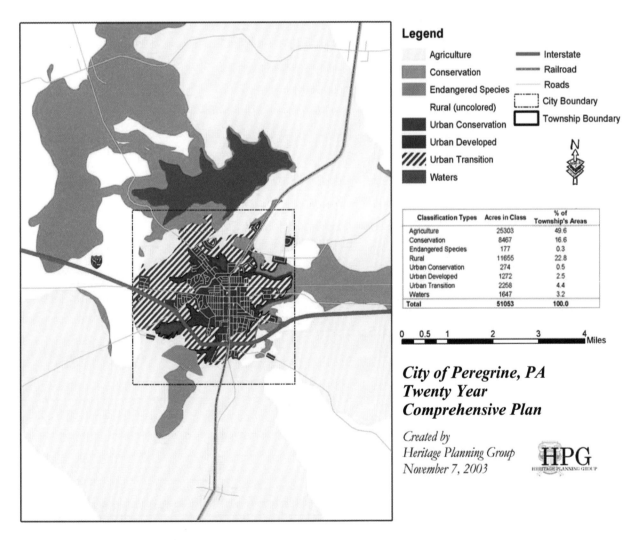

Legend

Agriculture		Interstate	
Conservation		Railroad	
Endangered Species		Roads	
Rural (uncolored)		City Boundary	
Urban Conservation		Township Boundary	
Urban Developed			
Urban Transition			
Waters			

Classification Types	Acres in Class	% of Township's Areas
Agriculture	25303	49.6
Conservation	8467	16.6
Endangered Species	177	0.3
Rural	11655	22.8
Urban Conservation	274	0.5
Urban Developed	1272	2.5
Urban Transition	2258	4.4
Waters	1647	3.2
Total	**51053**	**100.0**

0   0.5   1   2   3   4 Miles

City of Peregrine, PA
Twenty Year
Comprehensive Plan

Created by
Heritage Planning Group
November 7, 2003

HPG
HERITAGE PLANNING GROUP

Figure 3. Illustrative Areawide Land Policy Plan

Land Policy Districts	Acres in Class	% of Township's Acres	Allowable Density Du/Acre	
Conservation	17,776	34.0	Max. 1	Min. NA
Conservation critical	3,048	6.0	Max. NA	Min. NA
Rural	26,674	55.0	Max. 1/20	Min. NA
Rural community	300	1.0	Max. 4	Min. 2
Urban transition	1,759	3.5	Max. 10	Min. 2
Urban conservation	635	1.2	Max. 1	Min. NA
Urban developed	1,208	2.4	Max. 10	Min. 4
Total	51,400	100.0	-	-

Figure 4. Illustrative Attributes of Land Policy Districts

You should prepare to present your areawide land policy plan to a simulated informal meeting with the planning commission and citizens of the town (represented by other students). You will have ten to fifteen minutes to present your proposed plan, focusing on the mapped land policy scheme and implementation policies and explaining the rationale behind the plan. Expect your table of policy district acreages to be compared with that of other teams.

The suggested target limit for the text of your report is two pages, not including maps, figures, and tables.

Suggested Reading

1. Berke, Philip R., David R. Godschalk, Edward J. Kaiser, with Daniel A. Rodriguez. 2006. *Urban land use planning, 5th edition* (ch. 10, The plan-making process; ch. 11, The areawide land policy plan). Urbana: University of Illinois Press.

Supporting Exercise D
Land Suitability Analysis

Product: A map identifying locations that are suitable for selected land policy districts or land uses

In this exercise you will use ArcGIS and the Hypo City maps to identify locations within the planning area that are best suited to particular land uses. Suitability analysis can contribute to several land use planning tasks. It can assist in the assessment of existing conditions by identifying areas that are especially well or poorly suited to development and conservation. It can assist in areawide land policy planning through identifying areas where provision of infrastructure and services is feasible, where development constraints exist, and where land conservation is desirable. It can assist in communitywide land use design by identifying areas with the best potential for specific uses, such as commercial centers or industrial parks.

In this exercise, you will use ArcGIS to define suitability in terms of specific conditions you define as part of a query or Boolean operation (i.e., use common operators such as And and Or). This is a simplified approach but it is appropriate because we are not trying to assess comparative importance of different land uses. The approach also considers interrelationships among features.

ArcGIS can be used to query the Hypo City database to select all locations that have the combinations of attributes you wish to use to identify locations suitable for a particular land policy district or land use. Students who are familiar with ArcGIS's Spatial Analyst extension may wish to use its functionality to convert features to raster, use the reclass function to rank each type of feature, use the raster calculation function to create their own series of overlays with a weighting schemes, and generate a suitability scale that shows degree of suitability (see relevant section of chapter 6 in *Urban Land Use Planning, 5th edition*).

The suitability analysis approach to be used in this exercise will likely identify some land areas as being suitable for more than one use. In these cases, you will have to further refine your queries or make informed choices about which use should prevail. You are advised to think about and discuss your queries carefully and flesh them out in critique sessions with your instructors. Record your queries and the corresponding results, as you will go through several iterations.

Overview of Exercise

This analysis will be done with three GIS files (*landclass.shp, landclass.shx*, and *landclass.dbf*) that together make up a shapefile called *landclass*. The *landclass* shapefile has been created by overlaying the township-level GIS files listed in Table 10. As a result, each of the polygons in the *landclass* shapefile contains a value for all of the attributes listed in Table 10. These attributes will be used with ArcGIS's database query functions to select areas that satisfy specified land suitability conditions. You can also create your own composite overlay using a subset of the township planning area layers.

The basic steps are:

1. Open your ArcGIS map document.
2. Activate the *landclass* layer (Hypo Township composite map).
3. Build logical queries to define suitability for particular land policy districts (or land uses if used for the communitywide land use design exercise).
4. Create a new GIS data file based on selected records.
5. Create suitability map layouts.

ArcGIS Instructions

Step 1: Open your ArcMap document

Open ArcMap, select ***Open an existing map***, and click on ***browse for documents*** in the window. Navigate to the directory/folder with your saved ArcGIS map document (i.e., from Supporting Exercise A).

Step 2: Activate the landclass layer (Hypo Township composite map)

Add the ***landclass*** shapefile to your map document by using the ***Add data*** button to add it to the data frame. The ***landclass*** shapefile is located in the directory you created when you installed Hypo City files, as described in the section of Part I titled "Installation."

Step 3: Build logical queries to define suitability for particular land policy districts or land uses

The results of your suitability analysis depend on the combination of factors you specify using ArcGIS's query builder. For example, a query that selects all polygons that are in the floodplain could mean that all locations in a floodplain are suitable for a particular land use (e.g., conservation land). Multiple criteria can also be used. For instance, a query that selects all polygons that are either in the floodplain or have high slopes could mean that all locations that satisfied either condition would be suitable for the land policy district or land use being considered (e.g., conservation).

The following procedures should be used to build logical queries.

- Choose *Select By Attributes* from the *Selection* menu. This option is also available when your attribute table is open.
- Choose and double-click a *Field*, then single-click an *Operator*, then double-click a *Unique Value* in that order. Then click on the *Apply* button.

Note: If the value you want to use in the query is not in the *Unique Values* list, click on the *Get Unique Values* box.

Operators: The following operators can be used to specify relationships between fields and unique values in a query.

=	equals
>	greater than
<	less than
<>	not equal to
>=	greater than or equal to
<=	less than or equal to
( )	expressions enclosed in parentheses are evaluated first
And	both expressions are true; e.g., "SEWERBUF" <= '1-2 mile' And "DEVELOP" = 'Open Space'
Or	at least one expression is true; e.g., "FOREST" = 'Lowland-hardwood' Or "FOREST" = 'Upland-Hardwood'
Not	excludes; e.g., Not "FLOOD" = 'FLOOD-PLAIN'
Like	if you are unsure of case, use the operator Like, and not '='. If you are uncertain of spelling or just want to use a shorter string in your expression, use Like with wildcards.

To see if you're using proper syntax or if the criteria you've entered will select any features, click the *Verify* button.

Sample Queries:

The simplest database query selects all of the polygons that satisfy a single condition. For example, all areas that have slopes greater than 15 percent could be selected by entering the following expression in the query text box:

"SLOPE" = '>15%'

A more complex query could use the And operator to select all of the polygons that simultaneously satisfy two (or more) conditions. For instance, all areas that are *both* in the floodplain *and* are not developed could be selected with the following query:

"FLOOD" = 'Flood-plain' And "DEVELOP" <> 'Developed'

Alternatively, the Or operator can be used to select all polygons that satisfy either one condition or another. For example, all of the areas that are *either* in the floodplain *or* not developed could be selected with the following query:

"FLOOD" = 'Flood-plain' Or "DEVELOP" <> 'Developed'

Your screen should look like this in ArcGIS version 9.1:

The Not operator can be used to exclude. For example, all areas that are open space excluding those in the flood-plain or reservoir could be selected with the following query:

"DEVELOP" = 'Open Space' And Not "FLOOD" = 'FLOOD-PLAIN' And Not "FLOOD" = 'RESEVOIR'

In the examples provided above, the Or query would select more polygons than the And query. A combination of operators should be used to define very complex suitability conditions, if desired. End your query by clicking *Apply*. The status bar at the bottom of the ArcMap window tells you how many features are selected.

The corresponding map features should become highlighted (with the software's default selection color). From this point on, they will be referred to as the "selected set." These map features and the corresponding database records remain the selected set (on which all subsequent analyses will be performed) unless they are unselected or cleared (by using *Clear Selected Features* from the *Selection* menu).

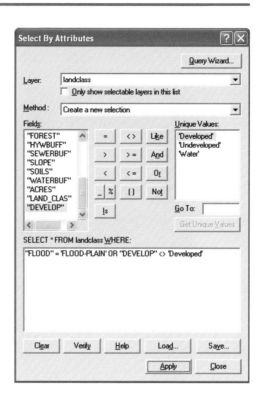

The database queries can also be used in different ways. For example, alternative suitability maps can be prepared based on the *number* of constraints (i.e., comparing the results of imposing one constraint, two constraints, and so on).

- Use *Add To Current Selection* to add the features or records selected in your query to the existing selected set. This option widens your selection and is equivalent to using the Or operator described above.

- Use *Select From Current Selection* to select the records from a previously selected set. This option reduces your selection and is equivalent to using the And operator described above. That is, only those features in a previously defined selection set that satisfy the new selection will remain in the selected set.

Step 4: Create a new GIS data file based on selected records

You may want to build a query and then save the selected features as a separate GIS shapefile. This new shapefile can then be added to the data frame's table of contents. For example, a new shapefile might represent land to be set aside for conservation. You can export features selected in your queries to create new shapefiles. To do this:

- *Right click on the layer name* in the table of contents, go to *Data*, and choose *Export Data*. Specify an output name and location for your new file.

- You will then be asked whether to add the exported data to the map as a layer. Select *Yes* for the option of making this new layer part of your current data frame's table of contents.

Note: Only selected features will be converted.

Step 5: Create suitability map layouts

Use the instructions in Supporting Exercise A to prepare any relevant map layouts. Save your project as another ArcGIS map document or as the same map document.

Suggested Reading

1. Berke, Philip R., David R. Godschalk, Edward J. Kaiser, with Daniel A. Rodriguez. 2006. *Urban land use planning,* 5th ed. (ch. 6, Environmental systems; ch. 11, The areawide land policy plan). Urbana: University of Illinois Press.
2. ESRI. 2001. *Getting to know ArcGIS Desktop.* Redlands, Calif.: ESRI Press.
3. Makczewski, Jacek. 2004. GIS-based land suitability analysis: A critical overview. *Progress in Planning* (62) 1, 3–63.
4. McHarg, I. 1992. *Design With Nature.* New York: John Wiley and Sons.

Supporting Exercise E
Computerized Land Policy District Classification

Product: A map of proposed land policy districts and a table showing the number of acres in each of these districts.

In this exercise, you will prepare a land policy district map as described in Exercise 3. The map should include at least the following areas: conservation, developed, urban transition, and rural districts. See Exercise 3 for the suggested color codes for each land policy district. These land policy districts are very broad and general. Student groups should refer to Chapter 11 in *Urban Land Use Planning, 5th edition,* for details on the five suggested tasks for creating an areawide land policy plan, for guidance on formulating location principles and standards for different land policy districts, and for a summary of the characteristics of various land policy districts.

Overview of Exercise

In this exercise, you will be using ArcGIS to create an areawide land policy plan. First, you will use ArcGIS to query the database to locate all areas with certain attributes that make them suitable as specific land policy districts. You could then determine the number of acres in these suitable areas and compare this total to the acreage needed to accommodate the projected urban growth. If these values agree, the suitable locations could be your first-cut estimate of the potential urban transition district. If the values do not agree, you may need to use other criteria to select more or less land until you are able to account for all the land needed to accommodate future growth. The basic steps for preparing the land classification map are:

1. Make a copy of the *landclass* shapefile to use in this exercise.
2. Review your attribute table.
3. Build queries based on the characteristics of possible land policy districts.
4. Assign desired land policy districts to selected polygons.
5. Compute total acreage for each land policy district.
6. Create land policy district map layouts.

ArcGIS Instructions

Step 1: Make a copy of the landclass shapefile to use in this exercise

The *landclass* shape file that was used in Supporting Exercise D will also be used in this exercise. Save a copy of this GIS data set and work with this copy to carry out the following steps.

Step 2: Review your attribute table

To open the attribute table for the *landclass* shapefile, right click on the layer name and select ***Open Attribute Table*** from the menu. The attribute table will open in a separate window within ArcMap. Scroll across the table and observe the field (column) headers. You will see that many of the fields correspond to the layers listed in Table 10. In addition, you will observe the following fields that have been added for use in this exercise:

- *Acres,* which contains the acreage of each polygon
- *Land_clas*, which can be used to store the land policy district category that you will assign to each polygon

The attribute table should look like this in ArcGIS version 9.1:

HYWBUFF	SEWERBUF	SLOPE	SOILS	WATERBUF	ACRES	LAND_CLAS
>2.5mile	>3mile	6%-15%	Good	>1320Feet	6.89	
>2.5mile	>3mile	6%-15%	Good	>1320Feet	0.25	
>2.5mile	>3mile	6%-15%	Good	>1320Feet	30.55	
>2.5mile	>3mile	0-5%	Good	>1320Feet	167.37	
>2.5mile	>3mile	0-5%	Good	>1320Feet	199.85	
>2.5mile	>3mile	0-5%	Good	>1320Feet	64.2	
>2.5mile	>3mile	6%-15%	Good	>1320Feet	12.79	
>2.5mile	>3mile	6%-15%	Good	>1320Feet	81.58	
>2.5mile	>3mile	0-5%	Good	>1320Feet	54.99	
>2.5mile	>3mile	6%-15%	Good	>1320Feet	347.59	
>2.5mile	>3mile	6%-15%	Good	>1320Feet	90.46	
>2.5mile	>3mile	6%-15%	Good	>1320Feet	430.05	
>2.5mile	>3mile	0-5%	Good	>1320Feet	477.85	
>2.5mile	>3mile	0-5%	Good	>1320Feet	324.68	
>2.5mile	>3mile	0-5%	Good	>1320Feet	180.96	
>2.5mile	>3mile	0-5%	Good	>1320Feet	11.86	
>2.5mile	>3mile	0-5%	Good	>1320Feet	32.93	
>2.5mile	>3mile	6%-15%	Good	>1320Feet	87.15	
>2.5mile	>3mile	6%-15%	Good	>1320Feet	232.7	
>2.5mile	>3mile	0-5%	Good	>1320Feet	262.59	
>2.5mile	>3mile	0-5%	Good	>1320Feet	352.39	
>2.5mile	>3mile	0-5%	Good	>1320Feet	210.73	
>2.5mile	>3mile	0-5%	Good	>1320Feet	104.47	
>2.5mile	>3mile	0-5%	Good	>1320Feet	7.11	
>2.5mile	>3mile	0-5%	Good	>1320Feet	11.99	
>2.5mile	>3mile	0-5%	Good	>1320Feet	118.38	

Attributes of landclass

Record: 0 Show: All Selected Records (0 out of 2351 Selected.) Options ▼

Step 4: Assign selected polygons to desired land policy districts

Now that you have selected polygons that meet the desired conditions for a given land policy district, you can use ArcGIS's data table functions to view the attributes for the selected polygons, assign values to these polygons, and summarize values to generate total acres.

To use the *Land_clas* field to assign a particular land policy district label to selected polygons, you must:

- Open the attribute table for *Landclass*. Click the **Selected** button (*next to "Show:" at the bottom of the attribute table window*). This should show only the records selected from your query highlighted in blue.

- Make the table values editable by selecting **Start Editing** from the **Editor** toolbar in ArcMap. Select the *Land_clas* field as the editable field by clicking on the column header. Make sure that you are working with the copy of the *landclass* shapefile (see Step 1).

Step 3: Build queries based on the characteristics of possible land policy districts

Use your knowledge of land suitability mapping (see Supporting Exercise D) to identify polygons that should be assigned to a particular land policy district. Save your queries for future reference.

The following is just one example of how to identify land that is not suitable for any development and assigned as a conservation policy district (e.g., prime agriculture use, water bodies, floodplain, current forest, slope greater than 15 percent, poorly drained soil, land more than 1,320 feet to the water resource).

Your query would look like this in ArcGIS version 9.1:

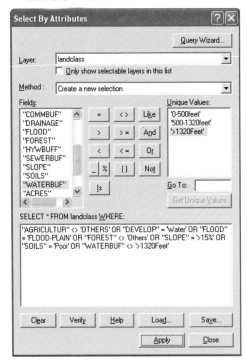

Note: If the Editor toolbar is not on your screen, go to the View menu (in ArcMap) and select Toolbars, Editor. Once you begin an edit session, the color of the label boxes at the top of each field (column) are displayed in white rather than in gray, indicating that the table values can be edited.

- Replace the labels for the selected records in the *Land_clas* field with the label for the land policy district to which they will be assigned. This is done by right clicking on the field header and selecting the **Calculate Values** option. You can then enter the desired label (in quotation marks) into the text box displayed on the screen. For instance, to assign all of the selected polygons to the conservation land classification, you should enter "Conservation" (using the quotation marks) in the text box and press the **OK** button.

- After you are finished, you can choose **Stop _Editing_** from the Editor menu to stop the editing process. You will be prompted to save your edits. If you are satisfied with your changes, select **Yes**. Click the **All** button at the bottom of the attribute table to display all records.

The attribute table should look like this in ArcGIS version 9.1:

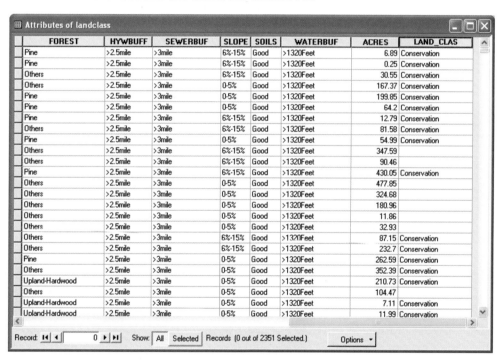

Step 5: Compute total acreage for each land policy district

Repeat steps 3 and 4 to assign land classification districts to each polygon.

The next step is to compute the total acreage that has been assigned to each land classification district. To do this you must:

- Use the summarize function. This is done by right clicking on the *Land_clas* field header and selecting **_Summarize_**.

- Select a field to summarize: **LAND_CLAS.**

- Choose one or more summary statistics to be included in the output table: choose to get the **SUM of ACRES**. (Click on the + box next to ACRES to open and select the SUM option.)

The screen should look like this in ArcGIS version 9.1:

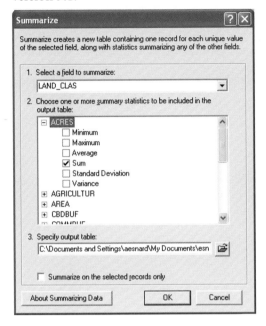

This will create a summary table in an output location that you specify. You can edit the table in Excel to change the field titles (e.g., change LAND_CLAS to "Policy District" and SUM_Acres to "Total Acres"), remove unnecessary columns (e.g., the "Count" value is the number of polygons and is included by default), and add your own columns. That table can be included on your poster as a summary of the total land area in each of the policy districts.

Step 6: Create land policy district map layouts

Use the instructions in Supporting Exercise A to prepare any relevant map layouts. Save your map document.

Suggested Reading

1. Berke, Philip R., David R. Godschalk, Edward J. Kaiser, with Daniel A. Rodriguez. 2006. *Urban land use planning,* 5th ed. (ch. 6, Environmental systems; ch. 11, The areawide land policy plan). Urbana: University of Illinois Press.
2. ESRI. 2001. *Getting to know ArcGIS Desktop.* Redlands, Calif.: ESRI Press.

Exercise 4
Creating a Communitywide Land Use Design

Product: A land use design for the Hypo City planning area to include a map showing the desired spatial arrangement of detailed land uses and community facilities in 2025 and explanatory text, along with a summary table of gross land demand and supply acreages allocated to generalized land use categories. A technical appendix (optional) can include the description of the process, suitability maps on which the design is based, and the calculations and assumptions for land supply and demand assessments.

The primary purpose of this task is to design a future physical environment to support the scenarios, visions, goals, and policies developed earlier in the plan-making process. Land uses in the land use design for the city planning area should be indicated in more detail than in the areawide land policy plan created for the entire township. At a minimum, the design should indicate the location of open space (perhaps several types); industrial areas; commercial areas of retail, office, and mixed uses; residential areas (including densities); and community facilities, including major roads and any other transportation facilities.

The text explaining the land use design should be brief, with a suggested limit of three pages, not including supplementary maps and tables. The text should focus on explaining the plan to citizens and decision makers, not on your technical planning process. Include in the text a summary table with gross estimates of land demand and supply acreages.

The land use design should be consistent with your scenarios, visions, goals, and policies; the areawide land policy district plan; your projections of population and employment; and any assumptions stated in previous exercises and included in preceding sections of the plan. It should be sensitive to environmental and infrastructure conditions. The land use design should be reasonable, but even more than the areawide land policy district plan, the land use design should not be a projection of trends. It is a design, not a projection. It should be organized around your concept of a desirable and sustainable future pattern of residential neighborhoods and activity centers.

The following points provide guidance on how to generate the products listed above:

1. Design scheme should be for your Hypo City planning area

2. Design scheme should be consistent with your direction-setting framework and areawide land policy district plan

   Review your direction-setting framework and State of Community Report, including issues, scenarios, and the vision statement, so that any proposed land use design standards and proposals can be incorporated into your design scheme. The following is an extract from Chapter 3 of the Davis, California, General Plan (City of Davis 2001) and shows the connection between design-related policies, goals, and standards:

   Example 1:

   Goal UD 1. Encourage community design throughout the City that helps to build community, encourage human interaction and support non-automobile transportation.

   Policy UD 1.1. Promote urban/ community design which is human-scaled, comfortable, safe and conducive to pedestrian use.

   Standards

   a. New neighborhoods shall be designed so that daily shopping errands and trips to community facilities can generally be completed within easy walking and biking distances.

   b. New development shall incorporate a balanced circulation network that provides multi-route access for vehicles, bicycles and pedestrians to neighborhood centers, greenbelts and other parts of the neighborhood and adjacent districts and circulation routes.

   …etc.

Example 2:

Goal UD 3. Use good design as a means to promote human safety.

Policy UD 3.1 Use good design to promote safety for residents, employees and visitors to the City
Standards

   a. Parks, shopping centers, schools and other institutional uses should be located on prominent, central sites where they will "belong" to the neighborhood they serve with strong pedestrian connections to these central sites.

   3. Design scheme should be based on design concepts and principles

   Chapters 10, 12, and 13 in *Urban Land Use Planning, 5th edition,* provide details on the sequence of steps that should be followed as you create your land use design:

   Task 1 — Derive location requirements
   Task 2 — Map locational suitability
   Task 3 — Derive space requirements
   Task 4 — Analyze holding capacity
   Task 5 — Design alternative spatial arrangements of land uses

   Open Space: refers to lands intended to conserve and protect valuable natural features and processes (e.g., wetlands and critical wildlife habitats). Rural and agricultural land holdings; natural hazards; and scenic, geological, ecological, and historic features can also be categorized as open space (refer to Chapter 11 in *Urban Land Use Planning, 5th edition*).

   Commercial and employment centers: refer to chapter 12 in *Urban Land Use Planning, 5th edition,* for details on essential components of employment areas and commercial and civic activity centers; their function, characteristics, and location and space requirements; standards (such as floor-area ratio and employee densities); and the space requirements and allocation to various commercial and employment centers.

   Residential community habitats: refer to chapter 13 in *Urban Land Use Planning, 5th edition,* for details on essential components of residential habitats (e.g., dwellings, supporting uses, circulation systems, open space); design concept models (e.g., neighborhood units, transit-oriented development, urban village); design principles and related standards (e.g., size, densities, walkability-distance criteria); and various steps in the planning process (e.g., estimating the number of dwellings required by the future population and allocating future required housing stock among proposed residential habitats).

   4. Sketching and mapping out a design scheme

We recommend that you first do a conceptual sketch of your land use design onto a hard copy of the parcels map. Use abstract symbols to indicate locations since actual sizes and shapes are not important for this type of conceptual sketch. See examples in Figure 5.

You should then:

   • Perform suitability mapping and assign land uses to specific parcels (see Supporting Exercises D and E, but work with the parcel GIS data file). Suitability maps might show, for example, the parcels meeting the combined criteria for employment centers, such as access to a nearby expressway system; appropriate physical characteristics (such as slope); and adequate utilities (including water and sewer).

   • Represent the land use design and calculate acreages of generalized land use categories (i.e., proposed design components will be grouped into general land uses) (see Figure 6). Instructions in Supporting Exercise F will allow you to lay out, review, and map different design schemes using GIS software.

Community Visions - Twin Silver Peaks

Urban Design

- Medium density
- Single-family attached
- Two to three story
- Garages in rear
- Animated street features

Mixed-Use

- Retail on ground floor
- Office above
- Animated streetscape
- Retain historic nature
- Width of sidewalk

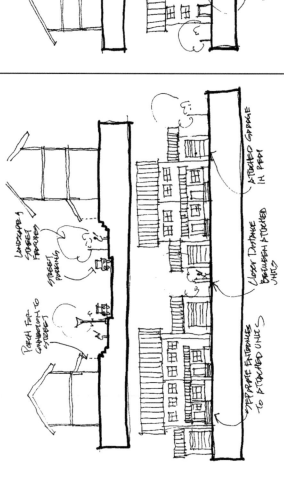

Figure 5. Illustrative Design Concepts

Cumberland, North Carolina - Neighborhood Design Concept

Cumberland should be comprised of neighborhoods and districts that aim to meet all needs (commercial, employment, residential and social) within walking distance.

Neighborhoods

- — All roads
- ■ E-School
- Park
- Green spaces
- Developed Conser
- Lake
- CBD
- Sewer Boundary

◯ Neighborhood

Figure 5. Illustrative Design Concepts

CITY OF CHARMANT, LOUISIANA

Concept Design Map - Bridge between year 2005 and the future

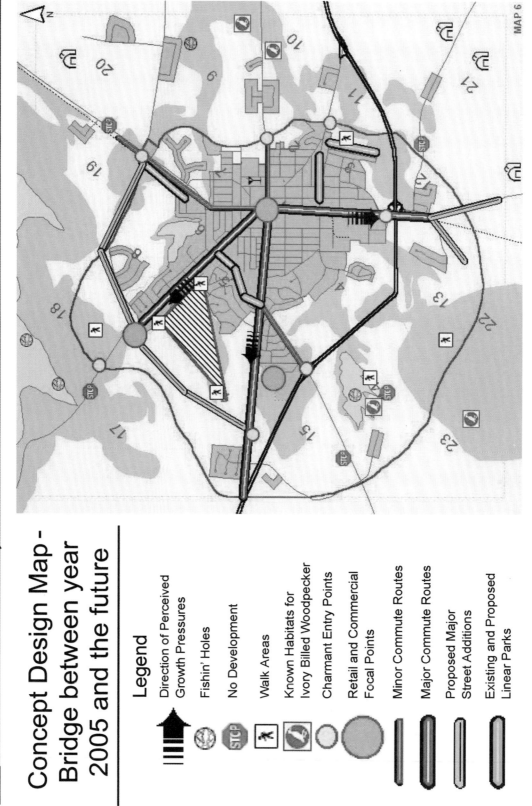

Legend

Direction of Perceived Growth Pressures

Fishin' Holes

No Development

Walk Areas

Known Habitats for Ivory Billed Woodpecker

Charmant Entry Points

Retail and Commercial Focal Points

Minor Commute Routes

Major Commute Routes

Proposed Major Street Additions

Existing and Proposed Linear Parks

Figure 5. Illustrative Design Concepts

Map 6. Land Use Design

Legend

- Existing Residential
- Existing Commercial
- Existing Cmty Facilities
- Others Cmty Facilities
- Open Space
- Water Body
- Future High Residential
- Future Low Residential
- Future Commercial
- Office Park
- City Boundary
- Hi-tech Industrial
- Industrial
- New Elem Schools
- New Jr-Hi School
- Community College
- Historic District
- Nature Reserve
- City Parks
- Recreation
- Future Greenways
- Pathways
- Interstate
- Railroad
- Road

0   0.25   0.5   1 Miles

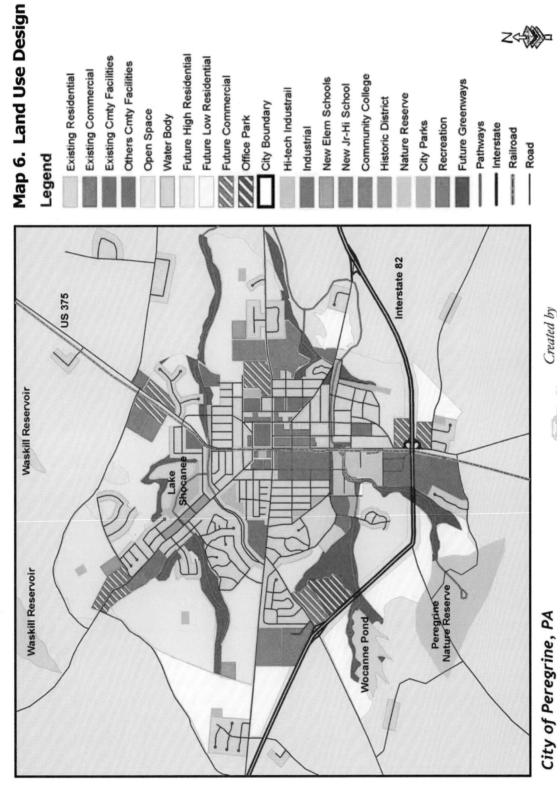

City of Peregrine, PA
Twenty Year
Comprehensive Plan

HPG
HERITAGE PLANNING GROUP

Created by
Heritage Planning Group
December 7, 2003

Figure 6. Illustrative Communitywide Land Use Design

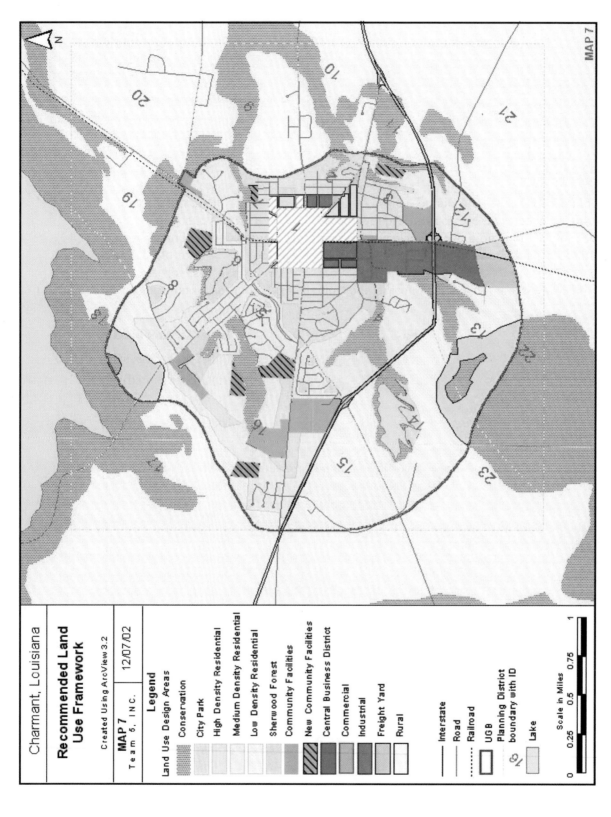

Figure 6. Illustrative Communitywide Land Use Design

General design issues to be aware of while preparing the land use design:

- The design should be treated as an iterative process. The design should be treated as tentative and subject to adjustments (perhaps generated by land demand and supply calculations) or other needs that emerge during the design process. We encourage you to use the following order when setting aside land suitable for future land uses (see chapter 10, *Urban Land Use Planning, 5th edition,* for logic and details):

  - Open space
  - Centers for industrial and office employment (including manufacturing, wholesale, trade, office, and service industries)
  - Commercial activity centers (including retail and population-serving office uses)
  - Other (regional facilities including airports, solid-waste facilities, and wastewater treatment and storage plants)
  - Community facilities (including libraries, schools, police and fire stations, train station, hospital)
  - Residential and supporting uses (including local shopping, recreational facilities such as concert halls, schools, circulation, smaller-scale open spaces, and other local resident-serving facilities)

- Every area should have an assigned use (including vacant parcels). One possibility for areas for which future use is uncertain or transitional is to designate them as rural or agricultural (i.e., general category of "Open Space"), with the understanding that these are holding areas to be given a more definite use in the future.

- Proposals to greatly expand the CBD may require radical changes in existing land use patterns. Unless there is extensive renewal and rebuilding at much higher density, any attempt to place 70 or 80 percent of commercial activity in the CBD in 2025 will necessitate invasion of surrounding residential neighborhoods.

- Highways do not make good borders to urban development, even though they show up visually as neat borders. In fact, highways will increase the accessibility of both sides of the road, including the side away from the city center, increasing the likelihood that what shows up as open space will actually be encouraged to develop in urban uses.

5. Land use color scheme

   The suggested color code for the land use design map is:

Shades of Green	Open space (including open space passive and open space natural)
Forest Green	Agricultural
Light Blue	Open water
Dark Blue	Institutional (including religious, government, education, and social and health care facilities)
Shades of Green/Blue	Recreational and cultural amenities
Shades of Red	Commercial/retail
Shades of Purple	Industrial (including light and heavy industrial)
Shades of Orange	Office (including mixed use)
Shades of Yellow	Residential (various types and densities)
Shades of Dark Brown	Rural and highway/convenience
Shades of Gray	Transportation
White	Vacant

6. Supply and demand calculations

An assessment of the present and future balance between the supply and demand of land for development and conservation needs provides a good foundation for any land use design. Although simple to state, this is a complex and difficult task. Realistically, the actual percentage of the land supply available for development at any time is constrained by regulatory limits, infrastructure availability, the willingness of owners to sell, environmental and physical limitations, and lack of market demand. Moudon and Hubner (2000) provide a good overview of land supply monitoring with GIS technology.

Supporting Exercise G presents one approach, with instructions for generating the following very basic land supply and demand summary table (Table 12). The previous version of this workbook used a more rigorous space allocation process, with a series of space allocation and accounting worktables for components of the land use design.

7. Identify whether there are strategic areas in need of more focus with a small-area plan (see Exercise 5)

Suggested Reading

1. Berke, Philip R., David R. Godschalk, Edward J. Kaiser, with Daniel A. Rodriguez. 2006. *Urban land use planning,* 5th ed. (ch. 4, Planning support systems; ch. 10, The plan-making process; ch. 12, Communitywide land use design: Employment and commercial centers; ch. 13, Communitywide land use design: Residential community habitats). Urbana: University of Illinois Press.
2. City of Davis, 2001. *City of Davis General Plan.* Davis, Calif.: Planning and Development Department.
3. DeChiara, Joseph, Julius Panero, and Martin Zelnik. 1995. *Time saver standards for housing and residential development,* 2nd ed. New York: McGraw-Hill.
4. De Chiara, Joseph, and Lee Koppelman. 1982. *Urban planning and design criteria.* New York: Van Nostrand Reinhold.
5. Jeer, Sanjay. 2001. *Land-based classification standards.* Chicago: American Planning Association. http://www.planning.org/LBCS.
6. MetroGIS. 2004. Minneapolis-St. Paul metropolitan area land use classification coding scheme/color scheme. http://www.metrogis.org/data/info_needs/existing_land_use/codescheme.pdf
7. Moudon, Anne Vernez, and Michael Hubner. Eds. 2000. *Monitoring land supply with geographic information systems: Theory, practice, and parcel-based approaches.* New York: John Wiley and Sons.
8. Perry, Clarence. 1929. *Neighborhood and community planning: The neighborhood unit.* New York: Regional Plan of New York and Its Environs.

Supporting Exercise F
Computerized Land Use Design

Product: A map of a communitywide land use design scheme

In this exercise, you further develop the areawide land policy district plan produced in Exercise 3 into a communitywide land use design. For example, urban-transition districts can be designed to accommodate high- and low-density housing, commercial, industrial, and office facilities (among others). See Exercise 4 for the suggested color codes.

Overview of Exercise

In this exercise, you will be creating a communitywide land use design map based on your planning policies, desired urban form, land use design principles, and the suitability of land for proposed uses. These functions, coupled with land supply and demand analyses (see Supporting Exercise G), provide one approach to design.

Step 1: Draw a conceptual sketch of your land use design onto a hard copy map of your parcels and the city planning area portion of your areawide land policy district plan.

Create a sketch map or conceptual sketch of your land use design onto a hard copy map of your parcels and areawide land policy districts. Other maps may also be useful (e.g., existing land use or roads). Use abstract symbols to indicate locations since actual sizes and shapes are not important in this type of concept map.

Step 2: Perform suitability mapping or select parcel polygons and assign a land use to them

If you choose to do a computerized GIS-based land use design, you should use the parcel lot lines to define boundaries for new housing, commercial, industrial, historic districts, parks, community gardens, and other polygon-type design components. The *parcel* shapefile is provided for this purpose. This file is located in the directory you specified when you installed the Hypo City files, as described in the section of Part I titled "Installation." The basic steps for selecting parcel polygons and assigning a land use to them are:

2a. Perform suitability mapping (see the instructions in Supporting Exercise D, but complete with the parcel GIS file). The **Select Feature Tool** functionality can be used to select polygons on-screen.

2b. Encode selected parcels with the relevant land use design component using the **Calculate Value** functionality and the LUDESIGN field. Remember that text (e.g., "Low density residential") should be entered with quotation marks (see the instructions in Supporting Exercise E, but complete with the parcel GIS file). Examples of land use design components:

  - "Greenway"

  - "Mixed use"

  - "Bus depot"

  - "Community garden"

  - "Hazardous zone"

  - "Junior high school"

  - "Office park"

  - "Apartment complex"

  - "Historic district"

2c. Encode the parcels with a generalized land use category using the **Select by Attribute** tool to select all LUDESIGN components that can be grouped into the following general categories. Note: The following queries in parentheses are incomplete examples and are for illustration purposes only.

  - "Open Space" ("LUDESIGN" = 'Hazardous zone' OR "LUDESIGN" = 'Greenway' …)

  - "Commercial"

  - "Industrial" ("LUDESIGN" = 'Office Park' OR "LUDESIGN" = …)

  - "Residential" ("LUDESIGN" = 'Apartment Complex" OR " LUDESIGN" = …)

  - "Community facilities" ("LUDESIGN" = 'Junior high school' OR " LUDESIGN" = 'Soccer field')

  - "Recreational" ("LUDESIGN" = 'Community garden' OR "LUDESIGN" = …)

  - "Transportation" ("LUDESIGN" = 'Bus Depot' OR "LUDESIGN" = …)

  - "Water"

  - "Vacant"

  - "Others" ("LUDESIGN" = 'Historic district' OR "LUDESIGN" = …)

2d. Use the ***Calculate Value*** functionality and the *F_LANDUSE* field to encode or type in with the general land use category. Your text write-up should indicate the generalized land use categories and the various land use design components that they encompass.

2e. Complete the summary table to calculate the total acreage for the general land use categories (*F_LANDUSE*). Use the relevant instructions in Supporting Exercise E, but with the parcel GIS file.

Step 3: Draw new features and save them as separate layers

If necessary, you can use ArcGIS's drawing functionality to (1) create new layers with polygon, line, or point features; and (2) generate areas of these new shapes. Because the land use design is done at the city scale, you will want to display the parcel or city roads map in the background as a guide for your design. Users with XTools Pro or other versions of XTools can use a different approach.

The basic steps for drawing new features and saving them as separate layers are:

- Create a new layer to represent proposed land use design components.
- Draw shapes to represent proposed land use design components.
- Calculate the area (in acres) for the proposed land use design components.
- Create a land use design map layout.

ArcGIS Instructions

Step 3.1: Create a new layer to represent proposed land use design components

- ***Open ArcCatalog*** and locate your Hypocity folder. If your folder is not in the table of contents, click the **Connect to** button on the toolbar and navigate to your folder. Select it and click **OK**.
- Select ***File, New, Shapefile*** (in ArcCatalog). In the pop-up window, type in a name for your new shapefile (e.g., greenbelt), and select the feature type that you want to draw (e.g., polygon). Press **OK**. You will see your new shapefile added to your folder in ArcCatalog.
- Close ArcCatalog and return to ArcMap.
- Add the new shapefile to your table of contents in ArcMap.
- Select ***Editor, Start Editing*** to start an edit session. If the Editor Toolbar is not enabled, select ***View, Toolbars, Editor.***

Note: The Task and Target pull-down menus (in your toolbar) become enabled.
Make sure that the *Task* reads *Create New Feature* and the *Target* is set to the name of the shapefile that you will be editing.

The following screenshot (ArcGIS version 9.1) highlights some of these buttons:

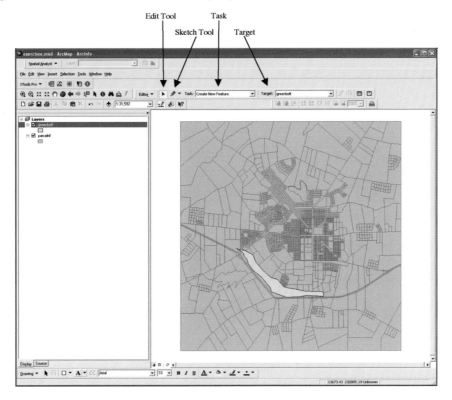

Step 3.2: Draw shapes to represent proposed land use design components

Note: If this is your first time using this functionality, you may need to practice several times.

The **Sketch** tool (the pencil icon to the right of the Editor menu) should be used to draw new features (see screenshot above). Only shapes with the specified feature type of the layer (polygon, line, or point) can be drawn.

- To start drawing a feature, click on the sketch tool icon (a crosshair appears on your screen if you move your mouse around).
- Draw the shape. To do this, click once to begin the shape and click once each time to add a vertex. Complete/close your polygon with a double-click.
- Use the **Edit** tool to select features for making changes.
- Choose **Stop Editing** from the **Editor** menu when you are finished.
- Set the data frame's map units to inches (if not already set that way).

Step 3.3: Calculate the area (in acres) for the proposed land use design components

A new record will be added for each new shape sketched. For example, if your new layer represents proposed school districts, each record might represent one of these districts as an individual polygon shape.

- Open the attribute table for the newly created layer by right clicking on the layer name in the table of contents. This table should have a *Shape* field.
- Choose **Add Field** from the **Options** menu and specify that you wish to add a field named Area to the table. Select LONG INTEGER, give it a PRECISION OF 10 (corresponding to the desired width of the field). Press **OK**.
- Choose **Start Editing** from the **Editor** menu.

- Select the Area field you just added.
- Right click and select **Calculate Values** from the drop-down menu. In the window, **check the Advanced box** and type in the following script (as shown):

Dim s.b. dbI Area as double

Dim pArea as IArea

Set pArea = [Shape]

s.b. dbI Area = pArea.area

- Type the variable *s.b. dbI Area* in the text box directly under the area = field name.

Area = s.b. dbI Area

Click **OK**. The area for the field will be calculated automatically, but in whatever map units have been specified for the view. In this case, your map units are inches (making the default area square inches).

Step 3.4: Convert area (in square inches) to acres

- Add a new field named Acres (LONG INTEGER and PRECISION of 5 is suggested). Highlight this new field and then use the *Calculate Values* option to enter the expression:

[Area]/(12*12*43560)

since there are 43,560 square feet in an acre and 12 inches per foot.

Your attribute table should now have at least four fields—FID, shape, area, and acres. You can continue building the database with new fields and additional data for your purposes.

Step 3.5: Prepare land use design map layout

- Use the instructions in Supporting Exercise A to prepare one or more map layouts.
- Save your project.

Suggested Reading

1. Berke, Philip R., David R. Godschalk, Edward J. Kaiser, with Daniel A. Rodriguez. 2006. *Urban land use planning,* 5th ed. (ch. 4, Planning support systems; ch. 10, The plan-making process; ch. 12, Communitywide land use design: Employment and commercial centers; ch. 13, Communitywide land use design: Residential community habitats). Urbana: University of Illinois Press.
2. ESRI. 2001. *Getting to know ArcGIS Desktop.* Redlands, Calif.: ESRI Press.

Supporting Exercise G
Land Supply and Demand Acreage by Generalized Land Use Categories

Product: One table that summarizes the space requirements for future land uses (demand) and for land set aside space for them in the land use design (supply).

The previous version of the Hypothetical City workbook used a rigorous space allocation process, with a series of space allocation and accounting worktables for components of the land use design. Chapters 12 and 13 in *Urban Land Use Planning, 5th edition,* make reference to that rigorous process.

This supporting exercise is a very basic land supply and demand assessment laid out in Table 12. It is meant to assist with finding a balance between appropriate locations and finding adequate space to accommodate future land uses. This table can be filled out manually or as part of a spreadsheet. A digital version of Table 12 (in Excel Spreadsheet format) is provided on the CD that accompanies this workbook.

Table 12
Gross Estimates of Supply and Demand Acreage by Generalized Land Use Categories

Open Space	Commercial Centers	Employment Areas	Residential	Community Facilities	Recreational	Transportation	Vacant	Water	Other	Total
A. Demand										
A1	A2	A3	A4	A5	A6	A7	A8	A9	A10	
B. Supply										
Existing Land Use (2005) – these values were generated using the GIS parcel layer and are slightly different from Table 5 in Part I of this workbook										
6232	71	122	905	66	112	125	26	126	22	7,807
Future Land Use (2025) – input values from product of Supporting Exercise F, Step 2										
C. Surplus (Supply-Demand)										

Note: The assumption is that the land use design covers the entire Hypo City planning area. If you want the land use design to cover only part of the planning area (e.g., for a small-area plan), then the acreage values for existing land use should be different and total less than 7,807.

A. Demand Values

Demand values are based on gross estimates of the amount of land required to accommodate the anticipated future population, economy, and environmental processes incorporated in the land use design. The following is intended to provide references and guide students on how to calculate demand values for columns A1 through A10 in Table12.

A1. Open Space

Standards are generally not relevant for open space intended to protect natural processes, avoid exposing development to natural hazard, or shape urban form (e.g., greenbelts and stream buffer areas). You should be guided by your areawide land policy district plan, where you have already mapped suitable areas for accommodating various types of open space.

A2. Commercial Centers

    a. Assume that commercial centers encompass retail space and population-serving office space. Refer to employment data (in Part I of the workbook or your revised estimates) for current and expected square footage needs.

    b. Use Tables 12-6, 12-7, 12-8, and 13-5 (in *Urban Land Use Planning, 5th edition*) for details on how to calculate acreage needs; OR

    c. Generate acreage from a researched and relevant standard on "square footage of retail space per consumer."

A3. Employment areas

    a. Sum manufacturing, wholesale, trade, office, and service industry employment (for 2025). Refer to employment data (in Part I of the workbook or your revised estimates) for expected employment in 2025.

    b. For this gross estimate, settle on a single density standard. Hypo City's employment density for manufacturing and wholesale is twenty employees per acre (see employment data in Part I of the workbook or use your revised estimate).

    c. Divide future expected employment by the density standard; OR

    d. Generate acreage from a researched and relevant standard on "acres of industrial land per employee."

Note: In areas under 100,000, such as the Hypo City planning area, a detailed breakdown by sector, type of employment center, and location is usually impractical and unnecessary.

A4. Residential

    a. Divide population forecast by household size to generate the unadjusted needed number of households/dwellings (see Table 13-3, *Urban Land Use Planning, 5th edition*).

    b. Adjust population upward to reflect the need to add vacant housing stock necessary for a housing market to accommodate residential mobility.

    c. Divide adjusted number of households by the residential density (refer to Tables 13-2, 13-3, and 13-4 in *Urban Land Use Planning, 5th edition*).

Note: Using one gross residential density estimate is not the best approach. Residential housing densities vary by location (central versus peripheral locations), development type, and age of development. Densities should also be guided by your direction-setting framework). Use of different density concepts (net density, gross density, or neighborhood density) has considerable space implications.

A5. Community Facilities

See section on "Community Facilities" in Part I of the workbook for school needs projected by the local government. A variation of these and other needs should be based on your land use design and direction-setting framework. For additional information on forecasting water, sewerage, and school infrastructure needs, see chapter 8 of *Urban Land Use Planning, 5th edition*. Table 13-6 (*Urban Land Use Planning, 5th edition*) provides useful standards for locating schools and the related area requirements;

    OR

Generate acreage from standards such as "acres of school site land per thousand population."

Note: For proposed new neighborhoods, the use of neighborhood densities allow sufficient space for such local serving facilities.

A6. Recreational

See section on "Community Facilities" in Part I of the workbook for recreational needs projected by the local government. A variation of these and other needs should be based on your land use design and direction-setting framework. Table 13-7 (*Urban Land Use Planning, 5th edition*) provides useful standards suggested by the National Recreation and Park Association;

    OR

Generate acreage from standards such as "acres of recreation land per thousand population."

Note: For proposed new neighborhoods, the use of neighborhood densities allow sufficient space for such local-serving facilities.

A7. Transportation

This can encompass space needs for pedestrian and bicycle paths, public parking lots, and other transportation services such as bus depots.

Note: For proposed new neighborhoods, the use of neighborhood densities allow sufficient space for such local serving facilities. Some pedestrian-friendly transportation facilities and amenities may also have been accounted for as part of the open space and community facilities categories.

A8. Vacant

This can be set aside for transitional land uses (such as evacuated disaster zones or brownfields) that are scheduled to be rebuilt but for which a future land use or time frame has not yet been determined.

A9. Water

Publicly owned water-supply reservoirs and watersheds should be categorized separately as "water." Like open space, standards are generally not relevant. You should be guided by your existing land use and buffer distance to reservoir maps.

A10. Other

This can encompass space needs for land uses that do not fit into any of the above categories.

B. Supply Values

Supply values are essentially the land areas committed to future land uses in the land use design. These values can be most easily generated using GIS. Complete Step 2 of Supporting Exercise F and input the total acreage values from the summary table into the matching cells in Table 12.

C. Surplus Values

This is the difference between supply and demand.

Note: Shortages of suitable land means that you will have to relax the standards of suitability, raise future densities, expand the planning area, or reduce the future level of population and employment that can be accommodated.

Suggested Reading

1. Berke, Philip R., David R. Godschalk, Edward J. Kaiser, with Daniel A. Rodriguez. 2006. *Urban land use planning,* 5th ed. (ch. 4, Planning support systems; ch. 10, The plan-making process; ch. 12, Communitywide land use design: Employment and commercial centers; ch 13, Communitywide land use design: Residential community habitats). Urbana: University of Illinois Press.
2. DeChiara, Joseph, Julius Panero, and Martin Zelnik. 1995. *Time saver standards for housing and residential development,* 2nd ed. New York: McGraw-Hill.
3. De Chiara, Joseph, and Lee Koppelman. 1982. *Urban planning and design criteria.* New York: Van Nostrand Reinhold.
4. Moudon, Anne Vernez, and Michael Hubner. Eds. 2000. *Monitoring land supply with geographic information systems: Theory, practice, and parcel-based approaches.* New York: John Wiley and Sons.

Exercise 5
Creating a Small-area Plan

Product: A small-area plan for one or more sections of the Hypo City planning area to include a map showing the area of focus as well as graphics or sketches that demonstrate desired spatial arrangements of detailed land use, physical design, and implementation measures.

Small-area plans share much of the nature of communitywide plans. The focus is on special areas within the community. Although small-area plans are best undertaken within a framework of a comprehensive plan, they may also be an appropriate response to immediate needs or opportunities, and might be undertaken in tandem with other components of the plan network rather than following the more comprehensive communitywide plan. Chapter 14 (*Urban Land Use Planning, 5th edition*) provides more details on the purposes served by these plans, types of small-area plans, plan-making processes, and illustrative content for a neighborhood and transit station area plan.

Products will vary based on the type of small-area plans (district scale versus neighborhood scale; urban development area versus environmental protection area). Examples include:

- Redevelopment area plan
- Neighborhood plan
- Transit stop area plan
- Historic district plan
- Business district plan
- Commercial area plan
- Natural resource area plan
- Business activity center plan
- Main street plan
- Transportation corridor plan
- Facilities complex plan

The text of the small-area plan should consist of the following:

1. A brief discussion of the existing conditions of the small area
2. A brief discussion of the future conditions of the small area
3. A short description of development-management techniques

The text explaining the small-area plan should be brief, with a suggested limit of one page, not including the map or the sketches. The small-area plan should be consistent with your goals and policies, the communitywide design, and any assumptions stated in previous exercises, and should be included in preceding sections of the plan. The small-area plan should explain its relationship to the communitywide plan and, if applicable, smaller-area plans within the area (see illustrative contents for a small-area plan in Chapter 14 in *Urban Land Use Planning, 5th edition*).

Suggested Reading

1. Berke, Philip R., David R. Godschalk, Edward J. Kaiser, with Daniel A. Rodriguez. 2006. *Urban land use planning,* 5th ed. (ch. 14, Small-area plans). Urbana: University of Illinois Press.
2. Kelley, Eric D., and Barbara Becker. 2000. *Community planning: An introduction to the comprehensive plan* (ch. 16, planning for particular geographic areas). Washington, D.C.: Island Press.

Historic and Redevelopment District Small Area Plan: Copper Valley

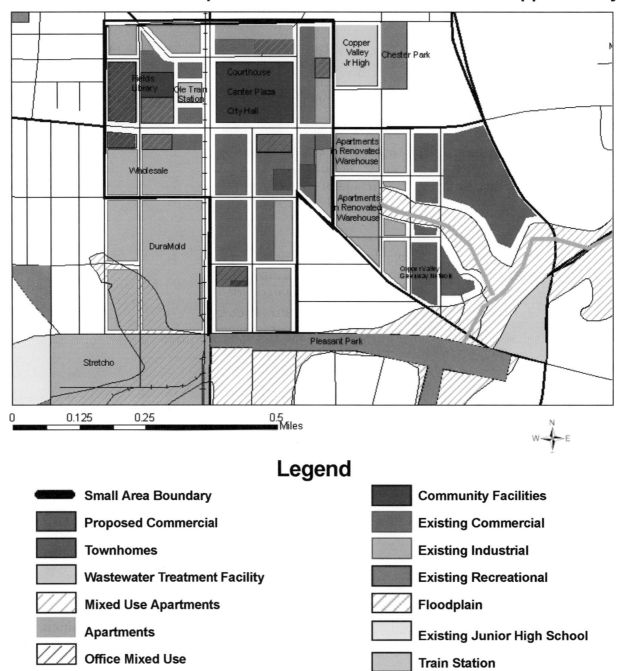

Legend

Small Area Boundary	**Community Facilities**
Proposed Commercial	**Existing Commercial**
Townhomes	**Existing Industrial**
Wastewater Treatment Facility	**Existing Recreational**
Mixed Use Apartments	**Floodplain**
Apartments	**Existing Junior High School**
Office Mixed Use	**Train Station**

Figure 7. Illustrative Small-area Plan

Exercise 6
Preparing a Development-management Program

Product: A proposed program combining regulations, public investments, pricing and taxing policies, and other actions that the community will implement to guide the development and redevelopment of Hypo City.

The development-management program should cover the content/type, location, timing/rate, and organization of the proposed development-management system. *Content* should describe each component of the system (e.g., a zoning ordinance and development-timing ordinance). A list or simple diagram showing how the components are parts of a coordinated program and how they are related to the goals listed in the direction-setting framework might be helpful, as shown in Figure 8. Each component should be described briefly in approximately one paragraph.

Location should specify where particular components of the development-management system apply. For example, it could include a generalized zoning map if a zoning ordinance is proposed, a map of sending and receiving zones if "transfer of development rights" is proposed, a map identifying major capital improvements, or a map of proposed annexation (see Figure 9).

Timing/Rate should specify the implementation schedule for implementing the various parts of the development-management program. For example, those areas where water and sewer lines are to be extended during the first ten-year period might be distinguished from areas where they would be withheld until the second ten-year period.

Organization should specify the responsibility for implementing the various components of the system. For example, you might distinguish between the county's implementation responsibilities and the city's, in addition to specifying agencies within the city that have major responsibility for certain components and where responsibility for coordinating the overall development-management program lies.

One student team prepared the following series of tables related to:

- Schedules (for conducting studies and inventories; for passing of regulations; for creation of programs and public entities; and for construction of public facilities)

- Task distribution (among various departments and agencies including the planning department, the public works department, the department of environmental protection, the opportunity finance committee, the chamber of commerce, the local historical society, and the school district)

- Funding source (including categories of general budget, tax incentives, impact fees, private sector, and grants)

The development-management program should be presented as a coordinated system, not just a list of devices. The best development-management practices seek to guide the future development of the jurisdiction toward long-term sustainability through the application of Smart Growth principles and livability criteria. Include a diagram or written explanation of the way the individual components supplement one another. The text should probably contain maps (e.g., areas subject to certain regulations or incentives, or provided with certain services) and tables (e.g., organizing the components of the development-management system or specifying who is responsible for implementation). Suggested length is four pages, not including tables, diagrams, and maps.

As an option, the development-management program may include a monitoring and evaluation approach to track plan implementation and to prepare for the next plan update.

Suggested Reading

1. Berke, Philip R., David R. Godschalk, Edward J. Kaiser, with Daniel A. Rodriguez. 2006. *Urban land use planning,* 5th ed. (ch. 15, Development management). Urbana: University of Illinois Press.

Figure 8. Illustrative Development-management Program

Goals (columns):

- G1. Preserve, promote cultural and natural assets
- G2. Link education, business
- G3. Promote commercial/retail zones
- G4. Partner for economic development
- G5. Enhance physical layout
- G6. Provide community facilities
- G7. Participate in regional transportation plan
- G8. Provide adequate, safe transportation
- G9. Provide alternative modes of transportation
- G10. Promote fair–share housing
- G11. Provide variety of housing types, prices
- G12. Minimize agriculture land conversion
- G13. Enable urban beautification
- G14. Utilize alternative energy
- G15. Promote awareness of environment and biodiversity
- G16. Revitalize urban core
- G17. Preserve historic architecture
- G18. Facilitate community access

Technique	G1	G2	G3	G4	G5	G6	G7	G8	G9	G10	G11	G12	G13	G14	G15	G16	G17	G18
Resource Land Preservation																		
Property tax incentives	●		●		●													
Transfer of development rights			●		●							●						
Purchase of development rights			●		●							●						
Acquisition of development rights			●		●							●						
Zoning for conservation												●			●			
Mandatory dedication of land	●											●						
Agri. and Forest Zoning																		
Special area protection	●											●						
Endangered habitat												●						
Critical area programs	●																	
Scenic view					●													
Rural Growth Mgmt.																		
Land acquisition						●						●						
Cluster development					●							●						
Subdivision regulations					●							●						
Rural land reassembly												●						
Zoning (inclusionary)										●								
Up/down zoning	●											●					●	
Minimum density zoning			●														●	
Maximum density zoning			●									●						
Tax free zoning			●															
Urban Containment																		
Jobs-housing balance											●							
Infill and redevelopment	●		●		●											●	●	
Urban design ordinance			●		●								●			●	●	
Neighborhood conservation	●																	
Adequate public facility standards			●			●		●	●								●	●
Facility Planning, Adequacy and Timing																		
Transportation demand mgmt.								●	●									
Growth phasing						●												
Carrying capacity								●										●
Impact taxes						●												●
Facility reservation fees						●			●									●
Developer exactions						●			●									●

Chickasaw, Mississippi
Capital Improvements Program

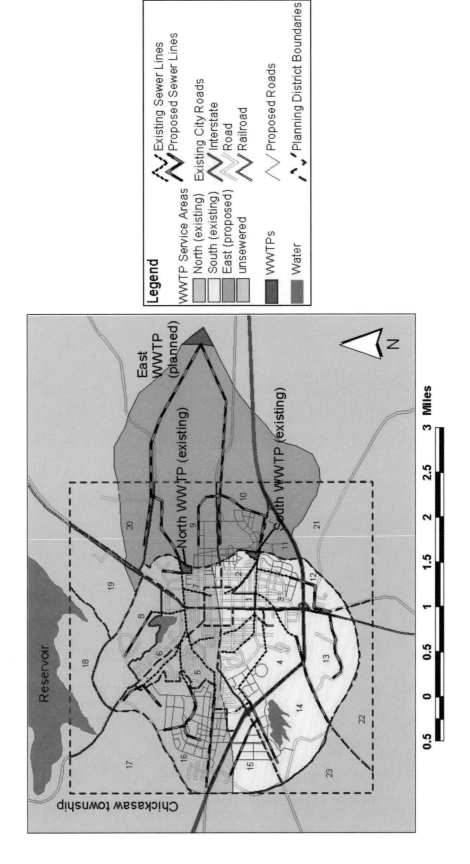

Legend

WWTP Service Areas
- North (existing)
- South (existing)
- East (proposed)
- unsewered

- WWTPs
- Water

- Existing Sewer Lines
- Proposed Sewer Lines

Existing City Roads
- Interstate
- Road
- Railroad

- Proposed Roads
- Planning District Boundaries

Figure 9. Illustrative Maps of Proposed Capital Improvement Plans and Annexation

Chickasaw, Mississippi
Proposed Annexation

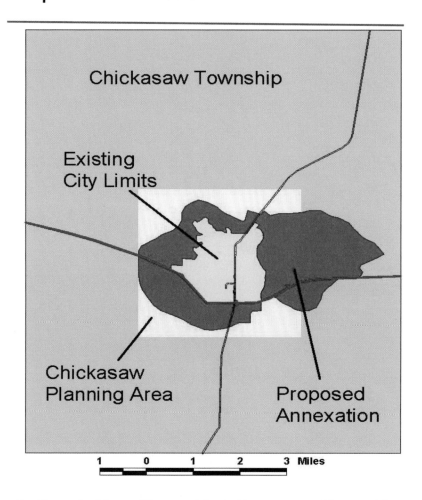

Figure 9. Illustrative Maps of Proposed Capital Improvement Plans and Annexation

Exercise 7
Evaluating the Plan

Product: A preadoption evaluation of the proposals of the future land use plan, including a public hearing and a city council review resulting in approval, modification, or rejection of the plan.

The bottom line for any future land use plan is its acceptance and adoption by the community. Otherwise, the cliche of a paper plan "gathering dust on a shelf" is accurate. To achieve community acceptance, a plan must be first reviewed and discussed by citizens, stakeholder groups, and elected officials. Many technically excellent and creative plans never make it through to formal adoption because they fail to be understood and accepted by the community.

The purpose of this exercise is to simulate the preadoption plan review and approval process through conducting a public hearing in which students play roles of various officials and stakeholders in order to evaluate one or more student-presented plans. Although instructors evaluate the technical soundness and overall public-interest content of the plans, the public hearing provides a different type of perspective. Stakeholders and politicians evaluate the plan proposals in light of their individual interests and aspirations and suggest revisions, acceptance, or rejection accordingly. Instructions for conducting the community review are given in Supporting Exercise H.

At the conclusion of the hearing, a council vote is taken to decide the fate of the plans evaluated. This is followed by a general election, in which council members are voted upon by participating stakeholders. Winning council members tend to be those who were most sympathetic to the largest number of stakeholders during the plan evaluation process. While necessarily compressed and simplified, this simulated community process forces the planner to consider the impacts of land use proposals on a variety of stakeholders.

As an additional option, technical evaluations of alternative plans may be conducted (particularly if the Hypo City setting is the same for all teams). The method selected will depend on the time and resources available for the evaluation. The simpler methods, such as visual comparison and numerical indicators, are the least demanding and may be the most feasible. For example, visual comparison could focus on desired aspects of alternative land use patterns, such as the compactness of urban areas, the connectedness of open space patches, and the accessibility of employment concentrations.

Numerical indicators could be compared for such things as the number of acres proposed for, and severity of constraints within, conservation-use areas (indicating relative impacts on property rights and hence the legal feasibility of alternative plans) and the number of new planning staff members needed to carry out the proposed development-management program (indicating budgetary feasibility of more sophisticated implementation techniques, such as transfer of development rights). Should the user have access to technical models, such as air- or water-quality impact models, these could also be used to evaluate alternative plans. However, such models are not included in the material of this workbook.

Supporting Exercise H
Plan Review Public Hearing

Product: A community evaluation of the proposed future land use plan, expressed in a simulated public hearing, and a town council election following official action on the plan.

This exercise simulates the preadoption public review process for the proposed land use plan. Although much of the plan preparation has been done in isolation from the public arena in which decisions are actually made, real land use plans are shaped by political and institutional structures and processes. This role-playing exercise gives the student planner an opportunity to experience and be involved in a mock political process in which many of the political dynamics of actual land use disputes can be constructively approximated.

The exercise consists of a public hearing before a town council and mayor on one or more proposed land use plans. Students play roles as interest-group representatives who have reviewed the plan proposals and want to express their opinions about them in order to sway the council vote. Other students play roles as elected officials and town planning staff members or planning consultants. Following council action on the proposed plan or plans, an election is held to select the next town council.

The objectives of the mock plan review and political process are:

- To enhance understanding of the inherent ethical and value dimensions of land use planning
- To highlight the incompleteness of purely technical approaches to land use policy
- To demonstrate the unequal distribution of costs and benefits among individuals and groups in the community resulting from land use plans
- To facilitate recognition and understanding of the power relationships that exist in local planning, which modify and constrain political outcomes
- To increase awareness of alternative political roles and functions the land use planner might assume, as well as roles of nonplanners and their impacts on political decisions
- To illustrate how political processes and institutional structures affect public decisions
- To point out the importance of intergroup and interpersonal relations and the types of skills and knowledge needed by planners for effective political action

Exercise Stakes

Plans confer tangible social and community resources. Proposed highway locations, lands designated for development or nondevelopment, and community facility sites distribute economic opportunities. Each actor in the power arena has a desired conception of the "right" allocation of resources and opportunities. The local political process mediates disputes over the distribution of these resources, weighing conflicting claims to arrive at acceptable land use policies. The balancing act may occur through dialogue, negotiation, and compromise or through manipulation, deception, and the exertion of raw power and resources. Each political context represents a combination of these factors, depending upon the social, economic, and political characteristics of the community at the time.

As a motivational force behind the role-playing exercise, each participant in the political process is assumed to be interested in achieving his or her individual objectives. Two types of objectives are built into this exercise, those of community interest groups and those of elected officials. It is assumed that each interest group will attempt, in every way possible, to advance its own particular goals and objectives. The group representative will seek adoption of the plan that best promotes its objectives.

A second assumption is that the mayor and members of the city council will act so as to gain reelection to office. While in reality elected officials are motivated by a number of factors (e.g., financial gain, peer pressure, altruism), constituent accountability is emphasized here. To ensure that elected officials are responsive to the expressed community interests, their role-play objective is to be reelected.

At the end of public consideration of the proposed plan or plans (and official denial, approval, or modification), a reelection vote will be taken. Before the vote, each council member will have an opportunity to make a brief campaign speech in support of his or her candidacy (no longer than two minutes). Each member of the community (class) will be allotted three votes. The three top vote-getting council members will be reelected and the candidate who receives the highest number of votes will be declared mayor. Voters are expected to choose council members who have been most responsive to their political objectives.

The Predecision-making Political Process

Hypo City has for several years been developing a comprehensive land use plan. The planning process has to this point been mostly in isolation from the public, with planners working on the basis of previously adopted goals and objectives and on what they feel to be consistent with popular opinion and the "public interest." The proposed communitywide land use design, small-area plan, and development-management program, just recently completed, are now in draft form and submitted for preadoption public review.

The proposed plan (or plans) is filed at city hall for public review (on reserve in the library or on a Web site). A date for public hearing has been set. Because of the immediate need for a planning guidance document, the city council has announced its plans to weigh the pros and cons of the planning proposals and make a decision the same evening. Council members have expressed publicly the urgency of resolving the land use planning issue and hope that some form of acceptable compromise among community interests can be arranged.

The proposed plan or plans will be chosen from among this year's draft submittals. All participants should acquaint themselves with the plan prior to the public hearing. More specifically, role players should read carefully the proposed land use design and development-management program in the context of their group's goals. These are likely to be the elements of the plan that receive the greatest attention in public debate.

Participants representing interest groups with similar goals may want to meet before the public hearing to discuss and agree upon joint objectives to be pursued in the political process. They can list, in order of priority, those plan components that are most damaging to or supportive of the group's interests. They can map out those plan items that the group would like to see modified or eliminated and those it wants to strongly support and protect. This list will serve as the group's action agenda in negotiating, bargaining, and lobbying in the political process.

Each participant should prepare a three-minute talk to present at the hearing. Flavor your talk with aspects of your assumed role personality. Following the hearing, turn in a written outline of your talk or your key points to the city clerk (instructor) for the official record.

The Public Hearing

Presentation by Planners. Prior to the decision of the city council, the planning proposal will be presented to the public for review and comment. A formal presentation will be given by the planners. They are the chief architects of the proposals and are thus the most qualified to present them. At a minimum, the planners will be expected to explain/describe the following:

- The basic goals, objectives, and policies guiding the land use design
- The major features of the land use design (e.g., location of residential commercial areas, sewer and water extensions, and highways) and the development-management program that will implement the design (e.g., major elements of the zoning scheme, programs for the phasing of capital improvements, and local taxing policies)
- The advantages and disadvantages ("pros and cons") of the proposed design and guidance system (presumably this discussion will be slanted toward the positive side)

Question Period. A formal period for questions pertaining to clarifications of this presentation will be allotted, first for city council members and then for members of the general public.

Statements by Interest Groups. Each individual will sign up at the start of the hearing for a three-minute time slot to publicly express his or her positions on the planning proposals (e.g., parts supported, parts opposed, parts to be modified). This will provide an opportunity for community interest groups to attempt to sway council members or other groups in the community. The mayor will call on speakers, keep careful track of the time, and halt comments beyond these time limits.

Determination of Consensus by Council. After the closure of the public hearing, the city council will determine whether the proposals—as submitted—adequately address or satisfy community needs. Each council member must weigh the political benefits and costs of voting for or against the plan(s) as proposed. At this point one of several things can happen: (1) the council can decide to vote on the plan(s) as proposed; (2) it can decide on alterations to the plan(s); (3) it can decide to adopt part of a plan, perhaps with some alterations, while postponing decisions on other parts; or (4) it can reject the plan(s). Adoption of a plan requires, according to the city's charter, the approval of a majority of the council.

If the vote is for approval, then this portion of the exercise has ended, and we move onto the reelections. This outcome, at least in the first round, is unlikely. Most groups in the community will have great concerns about the plan(s) as proposed and will be quite unfavorably disposed at reelection time to those incumbents who vote to approve them. If a majority are unwilling to vote for approval of the plan(s), a recess for discussion, negotiation, and the generation of alternatives may then be provided by a vote of the council.

This recess period shall not exceed twenty minutes, at which time the mayor must reconvene the council meeting. During this period, all groups and members of the community have an opportunity to exchange thoughts, propose modifications, bargain, build new coalitions, and so on. Council members are also available for informal discussion and negotiation.

At the end of the recess, the meeting will be reconvened and the business of plan adoption formally taken up again. The mayor will once again call for comments from the audience, and each group will be allotted an additional two minutes to state its case should it desire. The order of speakers will be reversed from that of the prior public hearing. This will provide an opportunity for groups to formally present new modifications/positions on the plan(s) to the city council, as well as to attempt to convince other community groups of the desirability of their proposals.

After all official comments are heard, the council may then offer official modifications to the proposed plan(s) (through motions) or vote again on the plan(s). The passage of motions to modify the proposed plan(s) is by majority vote. Once there are no further motions for modifications, the council may then vote to adopt a plan as modified.

Reelection of Council Members. Citizens now can express their approval or disapproval of the behavior and voting patterns of council members through the reelection process. After brief campaign speeches by council members, each participant will be requested to vote for three out of the five incumbents. Write-in votes will be permitted. The city clerk (instructor) will collect and tabulate the results and announce the winners.

Role Descriptions

Instructors will select the plan or plans to be evaluated during the hearing and will assign students to roles. The roles represented in the exercise will depend on the number of students available. Minimum needs are a planning team, a mayor, and council, and enough of the salient interest group representatives to provide a critical plan evaluation.

A brief statement outlining the value orientation of each interest group has been provided below. These are to serve as guidelines from which the individual role player, in concert with other members of the group, should act. However, it is up to the participant to determine which specific issues and positions he or she thinks this value perspective would support, based upon a searching review of the proposed plan or plans.

Although role players are expected to act to further their groups' interests, they should be open to adopting the views of other interest groups if their arguments are compelling enough or if they see value in forming a coalition with another group. To make the exercise most effective, individuals should separate their personal biases from those given in the role description.

Hypo Citizens for Environmental Integrity (HCEI)

HCEI was formed to combat the city's wasteful and sprawling growth pattern. Its concerns, however, extend far beyond controlling sprawl and include efforts to reduce air and water pollution and the consumption of agricultural, forest, and environmentally sensitive lands. Its members have supported reductions of auto usage in the city and the promotion of bicycle paths, pedestrian ways, and mass transit. In the face of large growth predictions, HCEI is distressed at the prospect that Hypo City will generally grow too quickly, assuming more than its regional share of the population influx and losing much of its rural and small town flavor. In the past it has lobbied for retention of natural resources and promotion of the park system. It has also argued for land use controls and public projects that reduce the probability of natural disasters (e.g., flood damage and contamination of groundwater through faulty septic-tank placement). HCEI has elicited support from a broad spectrum of the population, with generally equal representation along class lines.

Hypo Taxpayers Alliance (HTA)

HTA is concerned with encouraging public and private actions that minimize public taxation. Its members' efforts have focused on lobbying for public decisions that keep down local property taxes. They support land use actions that enhance the local tax base (e.g., loosening commercial and industrial zoning) and keep public revenue requirements at a minimum (e.g., providing only the most essential community services). HTA has also been active in keeping public fees and service charges low. They are supportive of the upper-income interests in the city and are spearheaded by landowners and homeowners concerned with the increasing costs of government. Although not generally supportive of most government programs, they are more receptive to those programs and services that are relatively efficient.

Hypo Citizens for Social Justice (HCSJ)

HCSJ is concerned with battling current social inequities and inequalities in the city. Its members have supported a number of public measures, from the provision of public housing to reducing discrimination in the hiring of city employees. In the past, they have been an effective political organization, commanding much of the city's black vote. In recent years, they have substantially increased voter turnout for the low-income and minority populations of the city. In the proposed land use plan, they are particularly concerned about the impacts that future growth policies may have on lower-income residents. They are anxious to see the benefits of future growth distributed evenly across all neighborhoods and income classes. Future community services and facilities, such as schools and open space, must be provided to poorer members of the community, as well as to business and upper-income interests. HCSJ is also very strongly interested in providing decent and well-paying jobs for lower-income residents, and will argue for future development policies that attract these kinds of industries and commerce.

Hypo City Chamber of Commerce (HCCC)

The HCCC is primarily concerned with promoting those land use policies that will benefit local commerce. Bringing new industry and jobs into the community and fully accommodating future growth are key aims for this organization. Although most forms of economic growth are favored, the HCCC is predominately represented by CBD retail merchants and tends to support the continued economic vitality of central businesses, generally favoring these locations for economic growth over more dispersed and peripheral locations. The HCCC supports government facilities and services that benefit the business community and that enhance the prospects for future economic and population growth. It has lobbied actively for the extension of sewer and water and the encouragement of upper- and middle-income homeowners (and thus a greater body of consumers). The HCCC is also ideologically opposed to most of the city's social and welfare programs and believes strongly in the American work ethic. HCCC members generally see little wrong with a land use pattern segregated by income.

Residents for Rural Living (RRL)

RRL members live largely outside the official boundaries of Hypo City in spacious country homes on large lots or farmettes. Many have moved to these outlying areas specifically to avoid the noise, dirt, crime, and other perceived unpleasant conditions of city life. They are primarily concerned with maintaining the aesthetic and scenic advantages of country life while also maintaining accessibility to city shops and services. Many of these homeowners are retired, and some are quite wealthy. Their central mission is to check the future development growth they fear is just around the corner and that will, they are afraid, destroy the beauty and charm of their surroundings. Many have also become hobby farmers, raising livestock and planting some crops. They are fond of claiming in public hearings that unchecked residential growth and development will have tremendous negative impacts on their farming operations. Many of these homeowners engage in limited farming so that they can take advantage of preferential property tax provisions. Bona fide farm owners are also represented in this group, although they are a substantial minority. Most full-time farmers resent the entrance of these new homeowners and particularly their adamant no-growth positions on rural development.

Landowners for Constitutional Planning (LCP)

LCP consists largely of residents (some absentee owners) who hold undeveloped land in the city's fringe. The prospects of planned growth and agricultural land preservation are disturbing and may result in substantial losses in their property values. Many of these landowners are presently full-time farmers, with tracts of land of considerable size. Others are speculators. All share a basic belief in the freedom of landowners to build unencumbered by government regulations, and in turn to reap the profits development will bring. They believe that legitimate land use planning is limited to private project site planning. This group is particularly fond of proclaiming that any land use controls of Hypo City are unconstitutional "takings" without just compensation. They are also fond of threatening to take the city to court and have done so on several occasions in the past. The farmers' arguments have been the most publicly accepted. They have charged that taking away their speculative value, in addition to being unconstitutional, undermines the economic vitality of the farming community. Without this property value, the collateral upon which they borrow (e.g., for expensive farm equipment) would be seriously restricted. Farmers also charge that the ability to sell off a lot or two from time to time affords them needed financial flexibility and "gets them over the hump" in marginal years. They balk at the thought of the government preventing a daughter or son from subdividing a new lot from their land and constructing a dwelling when the time comes.

Senior Citizens of Hypo (SCH)

Despite its meager resources, SCH has been instrumental in convincing the city council of the need for public services and facilities that benefit older citizens. In viewing the proposed plan, they will be cognizant of a number of factors, including the impact that proposed development and land use patterns will have on the lives of older residents; the impacts of community transportation facilities and services on the mobility of the elderly; the adequacy and location of existing and future elderly housing; the location and nature of other community facilities (e.g., recreation centers); and other services and problems that will impact older residents in some way (e.g., meals-on-wheels, dial-a-bus services, bicycle lanes, and community parks). They are also particularly concerned about encouraging future forms of economic growth that will provide supplemental employment for the elderly. In addition, because most members are on fixed incomes, they are generally worried about any potential increases in the local cost of living. Elderly residents in recent years have been a political force to be reckoned with, as their claims to resources have popular appeal. They have constituted a substantial factor in electoral bids.

Hypo Homebuilders Association (HHA)

HHA consists of residential builders and developers, although some members also build apartment projects, shopping centers, and office developments. They are interested in land use policies that benefit the building and land development industries. They want easy and cheap access to water and sewer systems, fast processing of permits, easy mortgage financing, and economic development that will bring more construction. They do not mind zoning, but like it to be flexible so that they can get it changed to suit what they want to build. They are against impact fees and other exactions, or "extortions," as they call them. They think the entire community ought to pay for streets, schools, parks, open space, water-supply reservoirs, treatment plants, and major sewer and water lines, not just the developers, new homeowners, and landowners. They want predictable land use controls and they cannot stand uncertainty or delays; "time is money," they say.

Hypo Renters Alliance (HRA)

Renters have in the past been underrepresented in the local planning process. Often they lack the cohesion and sense of permanence that homeowners have. Not only are they typically underorganized, but they are also infrequent voters, feeling that the outcomes of local elections will have little effect upon them. In more recent years, however, a concerted effort has been instituted on the part of this element of the community to organize themselves. They are beginning to view rental units not merely as transitional homes and are beginning to realize that even legislation geared to homeowners have substantial impacts on them. In years past, for example, council members have sought to keep homeowner taxes down by raising assessments on apartment buildings. This has in turn raised rents and encouraged apartment owners to convert to condominiums. Renters have also found themselves disadvantaged in other ways, as in the general bias of Hypo City government in providing community services oriented to home ownership (e.g., door-to-door trash collection, residential street subsidies). The renters are in favor of a more equitable distribution of community facilities and services, as well as more equitable approaches to paying for them. They are also convinced of the importance of encouraging the construction of new rental units and of providing areas of appropriate density for such rental housing.

Neighborhood Protection Leagues (NPL)

NPL consists of five neighborhoods, stratified socioeconomically around the planning districts shown in Map 20. Each neighborhood group is interested in promoting those political outputs that will best maximize neighborhood benefits. The northeast neighborhood, for example, has in the past been very active in lobbying for those transportation routes and linkages that facilitate easy travel for neighborhood residents, with little consideration of the impacts such projects have on other neighborhoods. Each neighborhood group is equally voracious in shielding off public projects or actions that are likely to impose substantial costs on its residents. The location of public housing, for example, is just such an issue—usually falling in the neighborhood or area the is least prepared to defend its interests. Because of the dominant position of single-family homes in Hypo City, home-ownership interests receive a considerable bias. Much of the aversion to public projects such as public housing or the proverbial sewage plant is because of the potential impacts these projects may have on property values. These groups are only marginally aligned with renters.

- Neighborhood 1: Central
- Neighborhood 2: Northeast
- Neighborhood 3: Southeast
- Neighborhood 4: Southwest
- Neighborhood 5: Northwest

Hypo City Planning Staff (or Planning Consultants)

The plan may be presented by the city planning staff or, alternatively, by planning consultants, depending on the plan's authorship. One plan may be presented or two plans may be offered for consideration. The planners have been working on the proposed land use plan for several years and believe strongly in its quality and balanced content. Although citizen input has been sparse, the staff feel that they have responded professionally to established community goals and objectives and the results of a communitywide questionnaire. Despite the planners' understanding of the controversial nature of their recommendations, they have faith that the professional quality and farsightedness of their plan will, once publicly presented, sway all opposition.

The planners should initially support their plan in the public hearing, but if substantial modifications are demanded, they are expected to assist in this process. Although they are initial advocates of their own plan recommendations, they also should recognize their obligation to facilitate discussion and compromise in the planning process.

City Council

There will be four council members and one mayor (with equal voting privileges). The mayor will preside over the hearing and subsequent council action. The primary concern of the council is to be reelected at the end of the exercise. This will measure their ability to master the political bargaining process and their skill in interpreting and dealing with constituent expressions. Although some politicians act on a commitment to the "public interests" or a sense of "ethical fairness," in this exercise, council members should follow the political self-interest model, seeking to maximize political support for reelection. To this end, no particular biases or political predilections are specified. Decision makers are assumed to be politically malleable.

Exercise 8
Producing the Complete Plan

Product: A complete future land use plan, including existing and emerging conditions; alternatives and scenarios considered; direction-setting framework; an areawide land policy plan (if prepared); a communitywide land use design (if prepared); a small-area plan (if prepared); and a development-management program, packaged into a unified report document.

Once assigned exercises have been completed, refined versions of individual exercise products should be compiled into a single complete future land use plan. At this final stage, the user should ensure that the various plan components fit together in logically integrated and consistently presented text, tables, maps, and graphics for edification of the plan reader. Assume that your audience consists of community residents and elected officials, who will refer to the plan in the course of decision making as a summary of adopted future land use policy.

This final version of the complete plan should contain a brief executive summary at the beginning. Along with an introduction, the executive summary should outline the issues addressed and explain the major features of the plan, the proposed future urban form, and the desired plan achievements. It should be followed by a table of contents and a list of tables, maps, figures, and appendices (see Figure 10). An attractive cover helps to present the plan positively.

The text and graphics should be arranged to facilitate reader understanding and plan usefulness as a planning reference document. Subheadings should be used to identify major sections and topics. Key points should be highlighted. Maps, figures, and explanatory tables should be integrated into the text in locations near the initial references to them.

Calculations should be placed in a technical appendix, where they can be consulted if necessary but do not intrude on the flow of the plan text. References, if any, should be grouped at the end of the text. A glossary can be added to define technical terms.

Supporting Exercise I guides the user through an evaluation of the future land use planning process. This is an opportunity to reflect on plan quality by checking through a set of criteria.

Supporting Exercise I
Critique of Planning Methodology and Plan Quality Evaluation Protocol

Product: A brief written assessment of the strengths and weaknesses of the land use planning process, based on reflections on the experience of completing the exercises, and an evaluation of internal and external plan quality criteria.

Critique of Planning Methodology

The critique is an opportunity to reflect about the planning process and techniques used in making a plan. This critique can be as short as one page or as long as three to four pages. The instructor might convert this exercise into an end-of-course, in-class discussion question.

The question to be answered is: What would you, the planner, do differently if you were to construct the plan over again or were given a similar task in a real community? The critique should be aimed at the planning process as if it had been carried out in a real-life situation.

Among the potential issues to be addressed in the critique are:

- How well did the planning process do in discovering and dealing with the important issues confronting the future Hypo City?
- Was the resulting plan an effective balance of social, environmental, and economic values?

Executive Summary
- Background
- Overview of Goals
- Conclusion

State of Community Report
- History
- Existing and Emerging Conditions

Community Involvement
- Town Visioning Meetings
- Identification of Significant Landmarks
- SWOT Analysis
- SWOT Analysis: Follow-up Meeting Responses

Direction-setting Framework

Areawide Land Policy Plan
- Description
- Developing
  - Urban Core
  - Increased Density
  - Transition
- Conservation
  - Large Park Reserve
  - Natural Hazard
  - Habitat Resource
- Rural
  - Rural Developing
  - Agriculture
  - Forestry
- Land Policy District Acreage
- List of General Suggested Implementation Policies
  - Urban Core
  - Transition
  - Large Park Reserve
  - Natural Hazard
  - Habitat Resource
  - Rural Development
  - Agriculture
  - Forestry

Communitywide Land Use Design
- Introduction
- Residential
- Open Space
- Commercial and Retail
- Industrial
- Community Facilities
- Land Use Design Process

Development-management Plan
- Studies and Inventories
- Regulations
  - Guidelines
  - Development Fees
  - Concurrency Requirements
  - Urban Growth Boundaries
  - Declaration of Existence of a Historical District
  - Construction and Renovations Ordinance
  - Design Standards for Signals and Urban Furniture
  - New Zoning Ordinance
  - Subdivision Regulations
  - Local Pollution Standards
- Creation of Programs and Public Entities
  - Environmental Protection Department
  - Mayoral Task Force for the Youth
  - Opportunity Finance Committee
  - Revolving Line of Credit for Local Business Expansion
  - Local History Education Program
  - Conservation Easements Program
  - Environmental Education Program
  - Environmental Monitoring System
  - Low-income Housing Program
- Construction of Public Facilities
- Funding Mechanisms
  - General Budget
  - Tax Incentives
  - Impact Fees
  - Private-sector Contributions
  - Grants

Appendix
- Maps
  - Descriptions
  - Map #1 Land Policy District Map
  - Map #2 Existing Zoning
  - Map #3 Existing Land Use
  - Map #4 Land Development Constraints
  - Map #5 River, Floodplain, and Forest Resources
  - Map #6 Prime Agricultural Lands and Forestry Resources
  - Map #7 Wastewater Infrastructure Conditions and Constraints
  - Map #8 Distance from Infrastructure and Services
  - Map #9 Existing Community Facilities
  - Map #10 Communitywide Land Use Design
  - Map #11 Future Zoning
  - Map #12 Future Community Facilities
- Tables
  - Table #1 Resident Report
  - Table #2 Land Classification Definitions
  - Table #3 Land Supply and Demand
  - Table #4 Schedule for Conducting Studies and Inventories
  - Table #5 Schedule for Passing of Regulations
  - Table #6 Schedule for Creation of Programs and Public Entities
  - Table #7 Schedule for Construction of Public Facilities
  - Table #8 Funding Sources
  - Table #9 Task Distribution

Figure 10. Illustrative Table of Contents. *Source:* Adapted from Hayseed, Indiana, Plan, 2002. Prepared by T3A Planning and Development Consultants (Joshua Abrams, Anthony Fusarelli, Juan Carlos Jimenez, Brian Mings, Adam B. Shindler, and Tama Tochihara).

- Does the resulting plan promote principles of sustainability?
- Did the technical analysis provide a workable foundation for the plan design proposals?
- What additional databases or technical tools would have been useful in preparing the plan?
- How could more effective public input have been incorporated into the planning process?
- How likely is it that the plan produced will facilitate a sustainable future community?

Internal and External Plan Quality Evaluation Protocol (adapted from chapter 3 of *Urban Land Use Planning, 5th edition*), discusses normative criteria to be considered in producing and evaluating comprehensive plans. Two key conceptual dimensions of plan quality discussed in *Urban Land Use Planning* are:

- Internal plan quality: involves the content and format of key components of the plan
- External plan quality: deals with the relevance of scope and coverage of the plan in fitting the local situation

Use the coding categories in response to the following questions. Compare your subtotals against the maximum score listed.

INTERNAL PLAN QUALITY CRITERIA (1-4)

1. ISSUES AND VISION STATEMENT

Coding Categories:
2 = Identified, detailed
1 = Identified, vague
0 = Not identified

1.1 Is there a preliminary assessment of major trends and impacts of forecasted change during future planning period? ____

1.2 Is there a description of the community's major opportunities and threats for desirable development? ____

1.3 Is there a review of the problems and issues currently or potentially facing local government? ____

1.4 Is there a vision statement that identifies in words an overall image of what the community wants to be and look like? ____

MAXIMUM SCORE: 8

SUBTOTAL ____

2. FACT BASE

Coding Categories:
2 = Identified, detailed
1 = Identified, vague
0 = Not identified

2A. Description and Analysis of Key Features of Local Planning Jurisdiction

2A.1 Present and future population and economy ____

2A.2 Existing land use, future land use needs, and current land supply for the future ____

2A.3 Existing (and future needs for) community facilities and infrastructure that serve community's population and economy ____

2A.4 State of natural environment, which represents valuable and vulnerable resources, and physical constraints to land use ____

MAXIMUM SCORE: 4

SUBTOTAL ____

2B. Techniques Used to Clearly Identify and Explain Facts

2B.1 Are maps included that display information that is clear, relevant, and comprehensible? ____

2B.2 Are tables that aggregate data relevant and meaningful to the planning area under study? ____

2B.3 Are facts used to support reasoning of explanation for issues? ____

2B.4 Are facts used to support reasoning of explanation for policy directions? ____

MAXIMUM SCORE: 4

SUBTOTAL ____

3. DIRECTION-SETTING FRAMEWORK

Coding Categories:
2 = Most
1 = Some
0 = None

3.1 Are goals clearly stated? _____

3.2 Are policies internally consistent with goals, and is each policy clearly tied to a specific goal (or goals)? _____

3.3 Are policies tied to a specific action and/or development management tools (e.g., vague policy: reduce flood risk vs. detailed policy: reduce development densities in floodplain)? _____

3.4 Are policies mandatory (with words like *shall, will, require, must*) as opposed to suggestive (with words like *consider, should, may*)? _____

MAXIMUM SCORE: 8

SUBTOTAL _____

4. COMMUNITYWIDE LAND USE DESIGN PROPOSAL

Coding Categories:
2 = Identified, clear
1 = Identified, vague
0 = Not identified

4A: Spatial Design

4A.1 Does plan have a future land use map? _____

4A.2 Are transportation/circulation needs considered? _____

4A.3 Are water and sewer needs considered? _____

4A.4 Are land use areas sized to accommodate future growth? _____

4A.5 Are proposed locations of land uses tied to suitability of landscape features? _____

MAXIMUM SCORE: 10

SUBTOTAL: _____

Coding Categories:
2 = Most
1 = Some
0 = None

4B. Implementation

4B.1 Are actions for implementing plans clearly identified? _____

4B.2 Are the actions for implementing plans prioritized? _____

4B.3 Are timelines for implementation identified? _____

4B.4 Are organizations with responsibility to implement policies identified? _____

MAXIMUM SCORE: 8

SUBTOTAL _____

4C. Monitoring

4C.1 Are goals quantified based on measurable objectives (e.g., 60% of all residents within 1/4 mile of transit service)? _____

4C.2 Are indicators of each objective included (e.g., annual percentage of residents within 1/4 mile of transit service)? _____

4C.3 Are organizations identified that are responsible for monitoring and/or providing data for indicators? _____

MAXIMUM SCORE: 6

SUBTOTAL _____

EXTERNAL PLAN QUALITY CRITERIA (5-8)

5. ENCOURAGE OPPORTUNITIES TO USE PLAN

Coding Categories:
2 = Identified, clear
1 = Identified, vague
0 = Not identified

5.1 Is the plan imaginative by offering compelling courses of action that inspire people to act? _____

5.2 Does plan portray a clearly articulated, action-oriented agenda (i.e., prioritized and flexible alternative courses of action that clearly identify overarching solutions)? _____

5.3 Does the plan provide clear explanations of alternative and preferred scenarios for community development? _____

5.4 Is the legal context that requires planning explained (e.g., meet federal/state mandates, identify top priority issues that need to be addressed to ensure legal defensibility)? _____

5.5 Is the administrative authority for planning indicated (council or planning commission resolution, state law, federal requirements)? _____

MAXIMUM SCORE: 10

SUBTOTAL _____

6. CREATE CLEAR VIEWS AND UNDERSTANDING OF PLANS

Coding Categories:
2 = Identified, clear and relevant
1 = Identified, vague
0 = Not identified

6.1 Is a detailed table of contents included (not just list of chapters)? _____

6.2 Is a glossary of terms and definitions included? _____

6.3 Is there an executive summary? _____

6.4 Is there cross-referencing of issues, goals, objectives, and policies? _____

6.5 Is plain English used (avoiding poor, ungrammatical, verbose, jargon-filled, and unclear language)? _____

6.6 Are clear illustrations used (e.g., diagrams, pictures)? _____

6.7 Is spatial information clearly illustrated on maps? _____

6.8 Are supporting documents included with the plan (videos, CD, GIS, Web site)? _____

MAXIMUM SCORE: 16

SUBTOTAL _____

7. ACCOUNT FOR INTERDEPENDENT ACTIONS
IN PLAN SCOPE

Coding Categories:
2 = Identified, clear
1 = Identified, vague
0 = Not identified

7.1 Are horizontal connections with other local plans and programs explained? _____

7.2 Are vertical connections with regional or state policies and programs explained? _____

7.3 Is a process for intergovernmental coordination for providing infrastructure
and services, protecting natural systems, and mitigating natural hazards
(flooding) explained? _____
MAXIMUM SCORE: 6
SUBTOTAL _____

8. PARTICIPATION OF INFORMAL AND FORMAL ACTORS

Coding Categories:
2 = Identified, clear and relevant
1 = Identified, vague
0 = Not identified

8.1 Are organizations and individuals that were involved in plan preparation identified? _____

8.2 Is there an explanation of why the organizations and individuals identified in the
plan were involved? _____

8.3 Are the stakeholders who were involved representative of all groups that are affected
by policies and implementation actions proposed? _____

8.4 Is there an explanation of participation techniques that were used? _____

8.5 Is there a clear explanation of how stakeholder involvement in plan is related to
prior planning activities? _____

8.6 Is the plan's evolution described, including effects of citizens and private
stakeholder groups? _____

8.7 Does the plan explain the support and involvement of key public agencies
(public works, economic development, parks)? _____

8.8 Does the plan incorporate input from a broad spectrum of stakeholders? _____
MAXIMUM SCORE: 16
SUBTOTAL _____

OVERALL MAXIMUM SCORE: 96
OVERALL TOTAL (Sum subtotals from 1-8) _____

Suggested Reading

1. Baer, William. 1997. General plan evaluation criteria: An approach to making better plans. *Journal of the American Planning Association* 63: 329–44.

2. Berke, Philip R., David R. Godschalk, Edward J. Kaiser, with Daniel A. Rodriguez. 2006. *Urban land use planning*, 5th ed. (ch. 3, What makes a good plan?). Urbana: University of Illinois Press.

PART IV

Notes to Instructor

We have worked with the Hypo City exercises over a number of years and found them to be a very effective way to help students discover the interesting complexities that underlie the process of preparing a future land use plan. The experiential learning and mental discipline afforded by grappling with interwoven planning decisions in an ordered sequence offer many similarities to the actual tasks of plan making in a practice setting. Producing a plan builds students' confidence in themselves as planners and rewards their efforts with a tangible product.

Workbook Background and Philosophy

This workbook has been designed to fill the need for a one-semester course in the craft of land use planning. Its exercises provide opportunities to apply the sequence of methods advocated in the textbook, *Urban Land Use Planning, 5th Edition*. It brings to life for students the sometimes abstract and dry materials of land use methods courses. It engages them in solving problems that they help to create, while giving them an underlying framework on which to work.

The Hypo City framework is value-neutral. It is a blank slate upon which different student cohorts may write their own planning stories, identifying the issues that concern them and proposing the solutions that appeal to them. The framework accepts the social, environmental, and economic issues of the time. It responds to planning goals aimed at sustainability, environmental resource conservation, social justice, or merely orderly development. Students may be as idealistic or realistic, as radical or conservative, or as laissez-faire or managerial as they wish. Comparing the resulting outcomes of diverse approaches enlivens everyone's learning—instructors' as well as students'.

Hypo City is a growing small town. As such, it simulates conditions found in many communities in the United States and elsewhere in the world. The small scale of the setting facilitates carrying out a variety of planning exercises leading to a complete plan. Students engaged in their first community plan-making effort can pull together a full plan in the space of an academic term.

The land use planning course at the University of North Carolina at Chapel Hill, Cornell and Florida Atlantic University assumes some previous student familiarity with land use issues, policy trends, and practice. Ideally, our students will have had the benefit of supporting planning and policy courses, quantitative methods courses, and GIS courses. But we always have some students who have not taken these and need to do outside reading or be coached by their fellow students. This lack of familiarity shows up most often during the completion of the development-management program exercise, when some students are unaware of the nature of basic regulations, such as zoning, and are mystified by more advanced techniques, such as transfer of development rights. Although we could offer the plan-making course later in our program, after students have taken more related courses, we believe it advantageous to provide it to students in their first year of graduate course work prior to undertaking a summer internship.

Our teaching approach is to mentor students within small, self-organized learning teams. Rather than a read/lecture/test format, we use a read/discuss/apply/critique/revise format. Frequent instructor reviews of individual team draft products during informal work sessions allow students to get feedback on their efforts and experiments in a nonthreatening, constructive process. Letting student teams revise their initial drafts up to the end of the course sets a tone of flexibility and acceptance of ongoing learning. Even though we grade intermediate products, including presentations, these grades are akin to performance indicators and the most important grade is given to the final plan as a package of the revised individual draft elements.

This present version of the workbook represents the evolution of our learning over many years, just as the student plans evolve each semester. The most recent changes in the workbook are listed in Part I of this workbook.

The workbook and the accompanying CD represent a considerable investment by the authors. We are pleased to make it available to others for advancing the cause of land use planning education. At the same time, we are aware that it would not be difficult to knock off pirate versions of the workbook and GIS data files and ask seriously that instructors prevent unauthorized copying and use by insisting that students purchase individual copies of the workbook.

Course Syllabus

Courses necessarily compress the tasks of land use plan making into an academic term. It would be possible to mitigate this compression by stretching out the content over a longer period or by dividing it among several courses. However, we believe that the benefit of a synoptic overview of the plan-making process gained in a single course outweighs the cost of dealing with a lot of material in a relatively brief time frame. In fact, the sense of a ticking clock and the inexorable intermediate deadlines help to move student decision making along at a reasonable pace, without allowing teams to become bogged down in endless debates over details.

We start our course with a short land use plan review or comparison exercise, which is not in the workbook. The purpose of this exercise is to ensure that all students have read at least two land use plans to gain a preliminary grasp of plan-making practice. Plans are selected from leading examples, including recent winners of APA awards. We also use some plans available on the Internet. At UNC, students are asked to compare two plans on the basis of the quality of their fact and value bases, design recommendations, implementation proposals, and presentation effectiveness, and to identify features worthy of emulation. Students can be asked to evaluate one plan based on internal and external plan quality criteria and to state lessons learned. This type of warm-up exercise could be dropped if students already have been exposed to land use plan content in previous courses or experience. Instructors can contact the authors for copies of the course syllabus.

Assignments

In addition to the various combinations of the basic exercises, the instructor has many other opportunities to revise or enrich the assignments. First, any combination of the supporting exercises may be added. However, both basic and supporting exercises can be tailored to fit available time and course purposes. For example, an instructor may wish to require either the areawide land policy plan or the communitywide land use design or the small-area plan.

Second, the instructor may revise the general approaches or specific techniques that are suggested in the exercises. Such experimentation often elicits deeper thinking about land use planning methods. For example, in Exercise 1, the instructor can change the information on housing conditions, the socioeconomic characteristics of the population, the future economic structure of the community (as reflected in the distribution of employment), or the environmental constraint maps. The city can be placed in different locations. Care should be taken, however, to anticipate domino effects on other aspects of the simulated situation and to maintain consistency among the various facets of the simulation. If such care is taken, the exercises are tolerant of modifications in the situation described, in the approaches taken in making the plan, and in the format of reports. There are no positively right answers, and the scale is too small to recognize slight inconsistencies among maps or between tables and maps.

Third, the products called for by the exercises may also be changed. For example, the formats of the plan components can be changed. Goals, objectives, principles, and standards might be required for only some land use sectors to simplify the exercise. The critique of the process and methods (Supporting Exercise I) might be converted to an in-class discussion. Many other modifications are possible.

We have tried a number of ways of assigning students to tasks. Depending on class size, instructors can use self-selected student planning teams of four to five people who remain together throughout the semester or mix students based on an assessment of interests and skills from presurveys. Four-person teams are ideal because they allow the work to be spread among several students. We always spend some class time discussing effective ways to organize and carry out teamwork, and we frequently have to counsel individual teams whose members have trouble staying on track.

We ask students to volunteer for assignments in the role-playing exercises, where the number of roles to be filled depend upon the number of students in the class. When choosing the plans to be presented at the visioning and public hearing sessions, we try to find those that will stimulate the most discussion or present the clearest comparisons.

Instructors should caution students that the exercises, particularly the communitywide land use design, will entail considerable out-of-class time. Students should be advised to complete a draft of each part of the exercises while it is being covered in the course and not wait until the last minute. In fact, we recommend that instructors require drafts of parts of the report on intermediate deadline dates—not for grading purposes but to provide feedback and ensure that students are keeping up. We give rapid-turnaround comments on drafts to encourage frequent updating and revision.

We recommend that students give oral presentations of the results of major steps in the overall Hypo City assignment. These presentations can simulate a variety of real situations. For example, sometimes we simulate alternative plan presentations by competing consultant teams to a Hypo City planning board or city council (a variant of Supporting Exercise H). We also simulate meetings with the public to formulate goals and identify planning issues (Supporting Exercise B). These occasions provide additional opportunities to explain and defend plan proposals and to get feedback from instructors and colleagues on the effectiveness of the presentations.

A Final Thought

This course can be quite rewarding for the instructor. You get to watch students develop a sense of the richness and challenge of land use planning. You are able to help them build their analytical, design, and communication skills. You can demonstrate the ethical dilemmas posed by the intersection of politics and planning. Each new class brings a different set of ideals and abilities and generates new creative versions of their imagined Hypo Cities. In short, it is a wonderful learning opportunity. Enjoy it!

Index

ArcGIS: boolean operators, 72; creating map layouts, 60-62; edit tool, 89; exercises and instructions, 59-62, 71-77, 88-90; generating area for new polygons, 89-90; sketch tool, 89; table summarize function, 76-77; terminology, 59

area: adding area field to attribute table, 89-90; conversion of square inches to acres, 89-90

areawide land policy plan: examples of land policy districts, 68-70; GIS exercise and instructions, 70-77; guidelines for creating, 68-70; product, 68

base maps: descriptions of, 15, 17-18; hard copies of Hypo City maps, 20-49; list of related GIS data files, 11

Charrettes: as part of community visioning meeting, 62

color codes for land policy districts, 68; for land uses in communitywide land use design map, 85

commercial centers: allocation of land for, 79; calculating supply and demand for, 91-93

community facilities: calculating supply and demand for, 91-93; existing, 11; map of public services, 41

community visioning: how to prepare and conduct meeting, 62-63; as part of workshop, 64-65

community-wide land use design: examples of land uses, 85, 87; GIS exercise and instructions, 86-90; guidelines for creating, 78-86; product, 78

data: employment, 7; existing land use, 10; housing, 6, 8, 12; installation of, 4; list of GIS data layers, 16, 19; population, 6; wastewater treatment capacity, 14

density: employment, 7; reference to standards, 92-93; residential, 9, 12-13

design. *See* community-wide land use design

Development-management Programs: guidelines for creating, 97-100; product, 97

direction-setting framework, 66-67

employment centers: allocation of land for, 79; calculating supply and demand for, 91-93

fields: adding to attribute table, 89-90

floor area: current office use, 8; current retail use, 7

focus groups: as part of community visioning meeting, 63

Geographic Information Systems (GIS): reference to hardware and software requirements, 4. *See also* ArcGIS

GIS data files: classification fields and categories, 16, 19; for Hypo City, 19; for Hypo Township, 16

goals: in policy framework plan, 66-67; definition, 66

Hypo City: base maps, 20-49; basic and supporting exercises, 3; current housing stock, 12; employment data, 7; examples of customized scenarios, 54-55; description, 5; housing data, 6; map units, 61; population data, 6

Incorporated City: description and boundaries, 5; extraterritorial planning and growth management jurisdiction, 5

installation: of Hypo City GIS files, 4

land policy districts: categories of, 68-70

land supply and demand: calculations, 90-94

maps: hard copies, 20-49

map units: for Hypo City GIS data, 61

meeting and workshop format: for community visioning, 62-63; for land use/development scenario construction by citizens, 64-65; for pre-adoption plan review, 64-65; participation techniques, 62-63

objectives: definition, 66; in policy framework plans, 66-67

open space: allocation of land for, 79; calculating supply and demand for, 91-93

parcel: maps generated using GIS data file, 19

participation techniques: examples of meeting format, 62-63, 64-65, 101-8; for generating vision statement, 62-63

plan quality: evaluation protocol, 111-15; external plan quality criteria, 114-15; internal plan quality criteria, 112-14

policies: definition, 66; in policy framework plan, 109

121

ANN-MARGARET ESNARD is the director of the Visual Planning Technology Lab and an associate professor of urban and regional planning at Florida Atlantic University. She has taught GIS and land use planning courses and has worked with geospatial information technologies for over a decade. She has written on a variety of related topics including quality of life and holistic disaster recovery, vulnerability assessments of coastal and flood hazards, and public participation GIS.

PHILIP R. BERKE is professor of land use and environmental planning in the Department of City and Regional Planning at the University of North Carolina at Chapel Hill. His research explores the causes of land use decisions, how these decisions impact physical environmental systems, and the consequences of these impacts on human settlements. His work in land use planning has been supported by the U.S. National Science Foundation; the United Nations Division of Humanitarian Affairs; the New Zealand Foundation for Research, Science, Technology; the Lincoln Institute of Land Policy; the North Carolina Water Resources Research Institute; and the Texas Sea Grant Program.

DAVID R. GODSCHALK, FAICP, is Stephen Baxter Professor Emeritus in the Department of City and Regional Planning at the University of North Carolina at Chapel Hill. He has been a planning consultant, a city planning director, the editor of a planning journal, and an elected town council member. Coauthor of *Urban Land Use Planning, 5th edition*, he has also written books on growth management, land supply monitoring, conflict resolution, coastal planning, and natural hazard mitigation.

EDWARD J. KAISER, FAICP, is professor emeritus of city and regional planning at the University of North Carolina at Chapel Hill, where he taught land use planning and quantitative methods. He has been department chairman; coeditor of the *Journal of the American Planning Association*; coauthor of *Urban Land Use Planning, 5th edition*; and has written on the application of land use planning to natural hazard mitigation and environmental protection.

The University of Illinois Press
is a founding member of the
Association of American University Presses.

_____

University of Illinois Press
1325 South Oak Street
Champaign, IL 61820-6903
www.press.uillinois.edu